# DEVELOPMENT OF SERICULTURE

# DEVELOPMENT OF SERICULTURE

**Prof. M. Lakshmi Narasaiah**
*M.A., Ph.D.*
**and**
*Co-author*
**G. Jaya Raju**
*M.A., M. Phil.*

*Department of Economics*
*Sri Krishnadevaraya University,*
*Anantapur—515 003*
*(Andhra Pradesh)*

**DISCOVERY PUBLISHING HOUSE**
**NEW DELHI – 110 002**

First Published – 1999
Reprinted – 2016

ISBN: 978-81-7141-466-6



**Development of Sericulture**

*Published by:*
**DISCOVERY PUBLISHING HOUSE PVT. LTD.**
4383/4B, Ansari Road Darya Ganj
New Delhi - 110 002 (India)
Phone: +91-11-23279245, 43596064-65
Fax: +91-11-23253475
*E-mail:* discoverypublishinghouse@gmail.com
sales@discoverypublishinggroup.com
*web:* www.discoverypublishinggroup.com

*Printed at:*
Infinity Imaging Systems
Delhi

# Preface

In majority of the developing nations, development efforts in the last decade were put on hold. In all the developing nations, poverty is on rise, economic growth has slowed down, employment has faltered and inflation is on upward swing. A greater proportion of the population in these countries depends on agriculture sector for their livelihood. But, in agriculture sector productivity is low. This is not only because of excess pressure on land but also agriculture in these developing nations is characterised by primitive technologies, poor organisation and limited capital.

Since the urban growth is severely limited, the growing labour forces have to get their employent in the rural areas or semi-urban areas in the coming decades. So, it has become compulsory for the agriculture sector to share the increasing burden since it is the major activity for the majority of the labour force.

It is obvious that in India larger than the necessary number of workers needed in agriculture are working on limited resources. As a result, agriculture sector has become an unprofitable activity with low levels of productivity. Moreover, the traditional crops have failed to absorb the growing labour force and to raise the incomes of the farmers above the subsistence level.

Since agriculture has been considered as the backbone of Indian economy, Indian agriculture can be broadly classified under two categories—(1) rainfed or dryland farming and (2) irrigated farming. Rainfed agricultre is primarily rain dependent. Rainfed agriculture in India supports 40 per cent of the total cultivated area. As irrigation facilities are inadequate, agriculture is still a gamble in the hands of monsoons.

For most of the irrigation projects, rainfall is the only source. Due to erratic nature of rainfall, most of the dams, tanks and other water reservoirs remain dry during summer season. These rainfed areas are frequently affected by periodic droughts, soil erosion, crop fluctuations and other related problems. To overcome these problems, the Government of India has implemented such projects which are helpful for eradication of poverty and unemployment and upliftment of the wearker sections.

In this context suitable strategies are needed to overcome the above mentioned problems. The discovery of productive employment opportunities in the integrated rural development assumes vital importance in the economic development of India. So, it is natural to start with agriculture as the biggest of India's Industries. The most important method of securing an increase in agriculture output is by inducing the cultivators to adopt better agricultural practices.

In fact, Indian agriculture now is no longer confined to the cultivation of traditional crops. The farmers are encouragd to take up agriculture practices which are integrated with live-stock culture, animal husbandry, dairying, fisheries, poultry, horticulture and sericulture to generate more income for each household.

In spite of the limitations in agriculture, it can be said without any doubt that Indian agriculture is on threshold of entering into a stage of development characterised by a shift from static technology to a modern technology, in which capital requirement and purchased inputs occupy large share. But, much of the success of new programmes will depend upon the ability of the workers who act as growth promoters.

It is in this context, sericulture with its vast potential for employment generation in rural areas plays a vital role in alleviating rural poverty. However, this is another crop enterprise which is identified as one of the most appropriate labour intensive cottage industries. This activity combines both agriculture and industry. It provides gainful employment not only at the stage of raising of mulberry plants but also at the stage of rearing of silkworms using output of the former as an input of the latter. Sericulture, for example, played a very important role in transforming the traditional bound Japanese agriculture into a modernised agriculture by intensive use of land, labour and capital.

Now, in India sericulture has become the most promising rural activity due to certain specific reasons like minimum gestation period, less investment, maximum employment potential and quick turnover of the investment. Sericulture generates direct and indirect employment in various ways. First, mulberry cultivation creates employment on the farm and secondly cocoon production which uses mulberry leaves as an input creates large-scale employment for the family labour of the mulberry growers, if that operation is also undertaken by the same household to reduce their underemployment in agriculture. Further, the reeling activity is also mainly undertaken in rural areas or semi-urban areas and the employment genereated there would help to reduce the rural unemployment in a significant way. In short, sericulture as whole, by its very nature of activities creates large scale employment and income generation opportunities in the rural and nearby semi-urban areas accelerating the economic growth of these areas.

***Authors***

# Contents

# Introduction

Agriculture forms the backbone of the Indian economy and despite concerted industrialisation of the last four decades, agriculture occupies a place of pride. Agriculture is the source of livelihood for over 70 per cent of population in the country.[1] In a predominantly agricultural economy like India, different regions have their own contribution for an overall increase in agricultural output and employment. Though it is showing a declining trend in the planning era, the share of agriculture in the total gross national product still remains high.

India is a developing country and the striking feature of its economy is the predominance of rural sector. The prosperity of a country depends on the prosperity of agriculture and allied occupations. Agriculture promotes economic development of the country. Economic development may be defined as transformation of an economy which is predominantly agriculture and traditional into largely industrial and modern. The economic history of many developed countries of the world like U.K., Russia, U.S.A., Germany, Japan etc., demonstrates that agriculture development helped and smoothened the process of industrial development by providing food raw material and employment. Historical records also clearly indicate that no country has attained take-off stage without first achieving a substantial gain in agricultural productivity.[2]

Accordingly, the discovery of productive employment opportunities in the integrated rural development assumes vital importance in the economic development of India. For proper utilisation of available manpower in rural areas, establishment of agro-industrial activities is one of the most suitable solutions. The integrated agro-industrial economy should be designed to embrace the entire development structure and process since agro-based industrial activities play vital role in providing productive employment to the rural manpower. These industries enjoy favorable linkages with agriculture and industry on the one hand and towns in the other. Hence, for rural development, small-scale agro-based industries with low investment would be most beneficial compared to other schemes.

In order to promote and encourage the already established agro-based industries, the Government of India has been implementing several programmes and projects like Drought Prone Area Programme ( DPAP) and Integrated Rural Development Programme (IRDP) etc.

The origin of the DPAP can be traced to the Rural Works Programme (RWP) taken up during the Fourth Five Year Plan period ( 1969-74). The RWP in 1970-71 was started in selected areas which were indentified as prone to drought on the basis of the objective criteria such as low extent of irrigated area, low and erratic distribution of rainfall and high periodicity of drought. These areas of our country periodically experience drought leading to the considerable loss of agricultural production and livestock wealth, besides causing untold misery to the people inhabiting in these areas. Large sums have been spent by the government for providing relief after occurrence of drought. Such expenditure has not helped to solve the basic problem of reducing the impact of the severity of the drought on the human and cattle population. Ecological deterioration, because of denudation of forests and excessive grazing, has led to soil erosion and decrease in the productivity of land. Because of the increasing population both human and cattle, even the marginal lands unsuitable for cultivation have been brought under the plough. The development of these areas is a challenging task and an attempt in this direction has been made by the government through the central scheme of DPAP.

Labour intensive schemes such as medium and minor irrigation, road construction, soil conservation, afforestation, fisheries were taken up under this programme.

The important objectives of the DPAP are :

1. To reduce the severity of the impact of drought.

2. To stabilise the income of the people.

3. To restore of ecological balance.[3]

The DPAP as such was started on the basis of the mid-term appraisal of the fourth plan and the report of the task force on integrated rural development set up by the Planning Commission. The programme was confined to those areas which were originally taken up under the RWP. In the State Anantapur, Chittoor, Kurnool, Cuddapah and Mahaboobnagar districts have been selected for implementation of the DPAP.

The main strategy of the programme is to maximise the production in good rainfall years and minimise the losses when the rainfall is not adequate. This is sought to be achieved by adopting soil and moisture conservation measures on a scientific basis, so that maximum utilisation of all available water in the area is achieved. The unit adopted for such scientific planning is the watershed. Five to ten watersheds of about 4,046 hectare each are taken up for comprehensive development. On the basis of the soil surveys and land use maps, areas suitable to various crops, pastures and afforestation are clearly indicated.

Introduction of short duration and drought-resistant, varieties of crops are to be promoted to cut down losses on account of inadequate rainfall or long dry spells during the season. Since the development of agriculture has obvious limitations in the areas, the farmers are encouraged to take up subsidiary occupations like animal husbandry, sheep rearing, poultry, horticulture and sericulture. Sericulture assumes greater importance in drought-prone areas. Among the many practices and crops suggested for commercialisation, sericulture is the most suitable one in drought-prone regions since it provides more employment opportunities per acre of its cultivation and ensures greater income to the farmers.

In Indian economy, agriculture is the dominant sector in employment providing work to 70 per cent of the population and accounting for 45 per cent of the GNP.

## 1. Importance of the Study

Sericulture is a cottage industry par excellence with its agricultural base, industrial superstructure and labour intensive nature. It is remarkable for its low investment, and quick and high returns, which make it an ideal industry or enterprise which fits well into the socio-economic fabric of India. Sericulture is highly recommended by planners and administrators as one of the most effective tools for rural reconstruction with development of the rural society.

Sericulture is a labour intensive industry in all its phases, namely mulberry cultivation, silkworm rearing, silk reeling and other post-cocoon processes such as twisting, dyeing, weaving, printing and finishing. The industry provides whole or part-time employment to more than 30 per cent are who drawn from the Scheduled Caste, Scheduled Tribes and other Backward sections. Till recently, sericulture was considered a subsidiary occupation. Introduction of new technology of sericulture has led to making the industry a highly remunerative crop,[4] as reflected in increasing acreage being brought under mulberry cultivation and the step-up in the raw silk output being witnessed every year.

Out of the 5,76,000 villages in India, sericulture is practised in about 50,000 villages providing employment to about six million people, most of them belonging to the weaker sections of the society i.e., silkworm seed producer, farmer and rearer, reeler/spinner, twister, weaver, trader etc.[5]

Before implementation of DPAP in 1975, the area under mulberry was only 1.214 hectares. It has now increased to 311,235 hectares by 1992. The financial allocation for sericulture development in the district has been increasingly every year from 5.20 to 57.28 lakhs by 1988-89. After that there was backward shift in financial allocation.

As a result of this rapid investment in sericulture practice in the district, naturally, some changes took place in the economic variables, mainly in the field of cost of production of cocoons. With the introduction of modern techniques in the sericulture, the demand for skilled labour has increased. High yielding variety of silkworm races have evolved as a result of continuous efforts of research institutions. Employment opportunities have been increasing and raising the standards of living of farmers who undertook sericulture practice a decade ago, are now in a position to maintain decent living. In addition to this, the involvement of house labour has decreased. Infrastructure facilities have increased to a greater extent. In spite of all-round progress in the sericulture activity in the district, marketing facilities are inadequate. Attracted by the fair prices of cocoons, the sericulturists usually go to the cocoon markets of Karnataka State for selling cocoons.

## 2. Need for the Present Study

The need for the present study arose mainly on account of the necessity to assess the development of sericulture in a drought-prone district like Anantapur and the conditions which forced the farmers of the district to take up mulberry cultivation in view of its opportunities and assured income to the farmers. The enquiry is also designed to find out the causative factors for the development of sericulture in the district.

There is considerable literature about sericulture in the form of monthly magazines, published reports, and information with the sericulture department. All these studies covered a wide range and so far no specific study has been made on the development of sericulture in Anantapur district, where sericulture is unique source of income to the retarded sections of the people.

This book aims:

1. To study the status of sericulture in India in general and Andhra Pradesh in particular.
2. To evaluate the origin and growth of sericulture in Anantapur district.
3. To analyse the causative factors for the development of sericulture in Anantapur district.
4. To highlight the problems faced by sericulturists in Anantapur district.

2

# Status of Sericulture in India

Sericulture today is a well established agro-based industry. It is an effective tool of rural development as it generates more income and employment. Sericulture industry today occupies a pride of place in the rural economy of the country. The final product of sericulture is silk. Silk can be produced and marketed where climate conditions are favorable and labour is cheap and abundant. Sericulture, in this way, is one of the most labour-intensive activities combining both agriculture and industry. In this chapter an attempt is made to present a detailed picture of the progress of sericulture in India and Andhra Pradesh.

Sericulture is an ancient industry in India dating back at least to the second century B.C.[1] According to some historians, raw silk was exported from India to Rome during the reign of Kanishka in 58 B.C. In its long history, sericulture has passed through periods of great prosperity as well saw decline.

Efforts where made in the 18th, 19th and 20th centuries, during the British rule, to patronise silk, mainly by the British traders. It actually flourished in the states of Bengal, Mysore and Kashmir. Then, sericulture suffered a series of setbacks, but briefly staged a comeback during the war period. When the Second World War ended in the mid-1940s, silk industry slumped as war related silk consumption ceased abruptly.

Thanks to the assistance of the Government of India and the measures it took to encourage sericulture in the country after 1945. This industry once again entered a period of prosperity. Sericulture took a rapid stride towards progress especially during the last two decades. And, since then it has come of age and is now poised for a great leap forward.

Silk is a way of life in India over thousands of years, it has become an inseparable part of Indian culture and tradition. No ritual is complete without silk apparel series, dhotis or shawl being used. Silk sarees from leading weaving centres are the only wear for women at any social or religious occasion.

The Indian silks are known for their fine quality, lustrous sheen and traditional colours. The masterly designed brocades of Varanasi, the luxurious creapes, georgettes and chiffons of Karnataka, the tie and dye crafts of Andhra Pradesh, Gujarat and Orissa, the delicate silks of Kashmir, sheet brilliant fabrics of Bandej and the temple silks of Kancheepuram, along with a host of other traditions of saris and other forms of appeal, are known world wide. In recent years, the tradition of woven fabrics has been joined by the more pragmatic prints from major printing centres in Bombay, Varanasi, Delhi and Bangalore.

## Fruits of Sericulture

A few years ago sericulture was considered a subsidiary occupation of poor farmers, while the big landlords used to cultivate only food crops, fruits, orchards etc. Now sericulture is no longer a subsidiary occupation and more and more farmers, including the big landlords, are taking up. The various advantages of sericulture already identified are as follows :

This agro-based cottage industry is so labour-intensive, employment creating and income generating that it is rightly called the 'kalpavriksha' or the 'kamadhenu' of the poor and down-trodden.[2] The other important feature in favour of this industry is its high profitability.

It has been found that sericulture is highly profitable as compared to many other crops. Mulberry has been replacing important crops in many regions of India, for example sugarcane in Karnataka, horticulture in Jammu and Kashmir, jute in West Bengal, grapes in Andhra Pradesh and several other crops.

Mulberry takes only six months to mature and afterwards four to six crops can be had in a year from the same plant which can stand for about 10-12 years. The leaves can be sold to silkworm rearers if the grower himself find it difficult to rear silkworms and sell the cocoons with better profits.

Sericulture involves simple technologies, easy to understand and adopt even by illiterate farmers and it gives returns in quick succession yielding income in every two or three months. Sericulture does not involve hard labour and rearing of silkworms is generally attended to by women and old people. Sericulture does not require sophisticated machinery and it involves use of simple appliances. Mulberry plants can be grown on any type of soil even in forest fringes, hill slopes and watershed areas. Sericulture ideally suits even in rainfed conditions because of its low cost of production and higher returns than any other crop. Mulberry plant withstands severe drought conditions and gives at least some income for sustenance while other agriculture crops wither away.

Sericulture would be a more advantageous industry for improving the economy of retarded section of the society like Scheduled Caste and Scheduled Tribes. Non-mulberry sericulture is largely practised by the tribals. Sericulture ideally suits for small and marginal farmers owning loss than one hectare of mulberry plantation. Sericulture provides self-employment to the educated unemployed youth in its different sectors. Sericulture also creates employment opportunities in the allied industries like manufacture of appliances, machines etc., raw silk produced has very good demand both in domestic and international markets. Thus, sericulture is a good source of earning foreign exchange also.[3]

## Silks of India

In strict sense, sericulture refers to the processes involved in production of natural silk. 'Serio' is a Latin word meaning silk.[4] Silk is a natural filament created by the silkworm. Therefore, sericulture means the raising or rearing of silkworms for production of silk.

There are four kinds of silk of commercial importance in the world i.e., mulberry, tasar, eri, muga. India has the unique distinction in the field of sericulture as it is the only country producing all the four varieties of silk. Silks are differentiated into these four kinds depending upon the race species of the worm and the food plants upon which they feed. The three kinds of silk tasar, eri, muga are called non-mulberry silks as mulberry is not the food plant for the worms. These are also called wild silks since the worms are not fully domesticated unlike mulberry worms and are practised in forests and hilly areas.

### Tasar Silk

Tasar silk is the product of secretion from the silk glands of Antheraca mylitta and Antheraca proylei, the tropical and temperate tasar silkworms, respectively. The tasar silkworms thrive on the three main food plants namely Terminalia tomentosa (Asan), T. Arjuna (Arjun) and Shorearobusta (Sal). Tasar is copperish coloured silk and does not possess the lustre of mulberry silk. In India the principal tasar producing states are Bihar, Madhya Pradesh and Orissa. On small-scale tasar culture is practised in Maharashtra, West Bengal and Andhra Pradesh. The oak tasar culture is now practised in sub-Himalayan States like Manipur, Himachal Pradesh, Uttar Pradesh, Assam, Meghalaya and Jammu and Kashmir.

Tasar silkworm rearing is practised by the adivasis and the tribals from the time immemorial in tropical bold, even much earlier to the introduction of mulberry silk in India. It is practised as a part of rich traditional culture. Unlike mulberry sericulture where 60 per cent of the cost of the cocoons accounts for growing of food plants, in tasar culture 14 million hectare of plantation in tropical and temperate zones are readily available for silkworm rearing.

## Eri Silk

The eri silk is also known as Endi or Errandi. It ranks first non-mulberry silk production. The eri silkworm (Philosamia ricini) thrives in India and is multivoltine yielding 4 to 6 crops a year. It is domesticated and the culture extends to an attitude of 5000 ASL in the hills. Its wild counterpart is found in north-eastern India. The eri worm feeds mainly on castor. Besides Kesseru, Tapieca/Cassava, Papaya, Payam and Barkessuru are also sometimes used. Eri cocoons are white and brick red in colour with shades, varying according to the fauna and plant used. The eri cocoons are spun since they are not continuous filaments and are open-mouthed. Bulk of eri silk is produced in Assam while on small-scale it is also produced in Bihar, West Bengal, Orissa and Manipur.

## Muga Silk

Muga is obtained from the worms (Antherea asamensis) which is quite similar to A. Mylita and A.Prolei. The muga silkworm is multivoltine producing 5 to 6 breeds per annum. This semi domesticated species is distributed and cultured exclusively in Assam. The cocoons of this moth are fawn coloured and hence the colour of the reeled silk is golden yellow. The caterpillars of the silkmoth thrive well on aromatic leaves of plants of som (Machilus bombycina kind) and Suolu (Litsea polyantha king). These are widely distributed in the valley of the river Brahmaputra.

## Mulberry Silk

What is commonly called as silk is the mulberry silk. It is produced by silkworm called Bombay mori and its varieties are found in all volutins. Mulberry sericulture is also known as mori culture. Mulberry silk dominates the field of sericulture in various aspects like quantity and quality of production and popularity. Mulberry sericulture is being practised in various states of India. It consists of four operations.

(a) Mulberry cultivation.

(b) Silkworm rearing.

(c) Disposal of cocoons and

(d) Silkworm egg production.

### *(a) Mulberry Cultivation*

Mulberry cultivation is purely an agricultural operation and a major factor determining quantity of production and hence the profitability of sericulture. It is the major cost factor and time and labour consuming activity though less skilled as compared to silkworm rearing.

Mulberry is hard plant capable of thriving under a variety of agro-climatic conditions. It respond well to the quality and efficiency of operations and leaf yield is also very high. Mulberry can be grown as bush, high bush, medium tree or long tree. Bush type is widely grown in South India. In Andhra Pradesh, mulberry is grown in bush form up to 1.50 to 2.10 mts. and exists from 10-12 years. Mulberry plant yields leaf within six months after the saplings being planted under irrigated conditions. Bush mulberry can be grown from cuttings, (seeds) seedlings and root-stocks. As it is a perennial crop, it needs manual attention throughout the year. The leaf yield of mulberry plant varies enormously basing on the inputs. It ranges from 3,000 to 10,000 kg. under rainfed conditions and from 10,000 to 40,000 kg. under irrigated conditions per hectare.[5]

### (b) Silkworm Rearing

Silkworm rearing is a cottage activity carried by the sericulturists in their own house or in a separate shed built for this purpose. It is the second major activity in sericulture requiring a lot of manual attention and becomes a complicated process when various technical and scientific aspects are to be understood and implemented for his productivity. It demands a substantial amount of managerial skills on the part of the rearer and his own experience forms a good guide.

*Silkworm Eggs*

Rearing starts with the purchase of silkworm eggs often called Disease Free Layings (DELs) or industrial seed. Thick paper sheets or cards on which the silkworm lays the eggs and are adhering to it. A laying occupies an area of about 2 square inches and about 400 eggs are present. The eggs colour varies from white to whitish yellow. Sericulturists buy DFLs from government grainages or licensed seed producers. Both multivoltine and bivoltine and even its cross breedings are used.

*Hatching and Brushing*

The eggs hatch within a period of 9 to 10 days after being laid. The egg sheets are kept in bamboo trays and when it is time for hatching the eggs turn into dark colour. At this stage rearers strike or shake the layings with soft feathers to initiate hatching. This process is called brushing. Tiny ant like worms (larvae) come out of the egg shells. These are very delicate. Each larvae crawl on to the tiny leaf bits. Then the egg card is turned upside down and the ants are left in the bamboo tray with an inlaid paraffin paper.

After brushing the real process of rearing begins. The larvae feed for about 24 to 25 days. This is the larvae stage. As the worms grow in size they are supplied with bigger and bigger leaf bits and are spread into a number of bamboo trays to prevent congestion and permit free feeding. Four to eight feeds are given in a day. These trays are normally arranged in a wooden stand placed one above the other with sufficient clearance for air circulation. During the larvae period, the worm moults 4 times. Moulting is the process when the silkworm casts off its existing skin in place of a new one. The duration of moulting varies from 20 to 30 hours increasing with age. In this period the worm stops feeding. The period before or after the moulting is allied in star. Thus, there are 5 in stars in the worms life. In the 4th and 5th in stars 90 per cent to 95 per cent of the mulberry feeding is given. While feeding, the worm excretes and this is to be cleared from the feeding baskets. Depending upon the climate the main factors being the room temperature and humidity the larve period varies from 23 to 26 days. The caterpillar increase its weight 10,000 times weighting 4 to 5 grams. A temperature of 25°C to 27°C and a humidity of 70 per cent to 85 per cent are considered ideal, decreasing with the age of the worm. The silkworm converts certain proportion of the food it takes into the silk substance and stores it in its body occupying 2/3 of the volume.

*Mounting and Spinning*

As the worm steps feeding they are transferred on to a bamboo tray called "chandrika", which has coiled bamboo strips, with one edge fixed to the tray. Through the mouth of the worm, liquid silk is exuded, with it, it forms a hammock sticking to "chandrika" to get an anchorage. It slowly moves its head ejecting the silk filament and spinning around itself, leading to the formation of the cocoon and its seclusion. The spinning is completed within 72 hours. The rate of rearing varies from 50 per cent to 80 per cent i.e., 50 per cent to 80 per cent of the eggs form into cocoons. Inside the cocoon the caterpillar undergoes metamorphosis and turns into pupa and later into the silk moth. This takes 10 to 12 days, the eclosion or the emergence of the month occurs on the 10th, 11th or 12th day. It comes out piercing one side of the cocoon. It is within this period the cocoon are removed and made ready for rearing. The harvesting of the cocoon is done on the

5th or 6th day of mounting. By this time cocoons become dry are ready for bulk transportation.

*Cocoon Yield*

These cocoon constitute the end product of the sericulture. The cocoon yield varies from one rear to the other, for every 100 DFLs the yield ranges from 25 kgs. to 50 kgs. The leaf consumption also varies from 450 to 900 kgs. with a leaf to cocoon ratio of 1:15 to 25. A rearer may have 4 to 6 harvests in a year by rearing 800 DFLs to 1,600 DFLs.

### (c) Disposal of Cocoons

Disposal of cocoons is minor activity but the sericulturist faces considerable difficulties in disposing of his cocoons. The disposal is bound by time factor as moths would emerge out of the cocoons after a certain time rendering the cocoons useless. The cocoons are sold at various government and private marketing yards and sometimes to middlemen and commission agents.

### (d) Production of Silkworm Eggs

Production of silkworm eggs is precarious activity and the seed organisation plays a vital role on which the success of the industry depends. The layings are called disease-free laying. Since care has to be taken, that the layings are healthy and free from any disease or infection after a microscope tests. The establishment where the layings are produced is called a grainage.

Normally the type of layings used by the rearers is a cross-bread layings produced from the multivoltine male Local Race (LR) and the bivoltine Female Race (FR). The FR and LR DFLs are also called basic seed and are produced by government grainages in their respective grainages. These DFLs are supplied to notified rearers for further multiplication. These rearers breed the DFLs and sell the resultant seed cocoons to the government grainages. In the CB (cross breed) grainages the commercial seed is produced by cross breeding.

As the moths emerge from the seed cocoons, the respective male and female moths are taken and put in moth funnels over a sheet of paper. After some hours of population the female lays the eggs on the paper. The moths are later discarded as they live only for short time. These layings are microscopically tested and only the healthy ones are sold to rearers.

Similarly pure bivoltine and multivoltine seed is also produced by hybridisation instead of cross-breading. Some licensed private seed prepares are also allowed to produce the industrial seed, and they are under constant supervision by the government sericulture staff. In Andhra Pradesh, the government has not allowed private producers. Thus, industrial seed production is carried in three stages i.e., (1) production of basic and seed in seed grainages (2) production of seed cocoons by sericulturists that is multiplication of the above seed, and (3) production of industrial seed from the above seed cocoons by government grainages or by licensed seed prepares.

## India and Other Raw Silk Producing Countries

India ranks second among the mulberry silk producing countries in the world. Sericulture in India has turned out to be a highly remunerative cash crop. It has been acknowledged as an important crop, particularly because of its potential for strengthening rural areas by providing more employment and increasing export earnings. The Table 2.1 shows India's place among other mulberry producing countries in the world.

China holds supremacy in raw silk producing countries. In India, production of mulberry raw silk is mainly confined to the States of Karnataka, Andhra Pradesh, Tamil Nadu, West Bengal and Jammu and Kashmir, which together account for about 98 per cent of the country's total mulberry raw silk

**Table 2.1 : Trend in World Mulberry Raw Silk Production**

*(Tonnes)*

| *Country* | *1983* | *1984* | *1985* | *1986* | *1987* | *1988* | *1989* | *1990* | *Total* |
|---|---|---|---|---|---|---|---|---|---|
| China | 28,140 | 28,140 | 32,000 | 35,000 | 35,800 | 35,800 | 40,700 | 46,400 | 2,82,680 |
| India | 5,681 | 6,895 | 7,029 | 7,905 | 8,455 | 9,683 | 10,905 | 11,487 | 68,040 |
| Japan | 12,456 | 10,800 | 9,592 | 8,341 | 7,864 | 6,862 | 6,078 | 5,720 | 67,713 |
| Russia | 3,899 | 3,999 | 4,000 | 4,009 | 4,000 | 4,000 | 4,000 | 4,094 | 31,992 |
| Republic of Korea | 2,292 | 2,088 | 1,850 | 1,650 | 1,608 | 1,608 | 1,200 | 1,200 | 13,496 |
| Brazil | 1,362 | 1,458 | 1,558 | 1,780 | 1,780 | 1,700 | 1,697 | 1,693 | 13,028 |
| Others | 2,770 | 2,720 | 2,671 | 2,874 | 2,874 | 2,874 | 2,285 | 2,285 | 21,353 |

*Source* : C.S.B. Silkman's Companion, 1992, Bangalore, p. 12.

production.[6] The table gives the clear cut idea about raw silk producing countries in the world.

**Mulberry cultivation in India**

The area under mulberry cultivation is gradually increasing in India. In 1980-81, the area under the mulberry cultivation was 1,70,000 hectares. Now the year 1990-91, the area under mulberry cultivation is estimated to be 3,13,109 hectares. That means over a decade the areas under mulberry increased by 184.18 per cent. The reeling cocoons and raw silk produced is also showing upward trend in production. The table gives clear cut idea on the mulberry growth in India.

It is seen from the Table 2.2 (Figure 2.1) that there was a gradual increase in the number of disease-free layings (DFLs) produced and the quantity of reeling cocoons. As a result of this, raw silk production also increased from 4,593 tonnes in 1980-81 to 11,487 by 1990-91. That is to say silk production was increased by 2.5 times over a decade. The quantity of silk waste also raised by about 3 folds from 1,376

**Table 2.2 : Growth of Mulberry Silk in India**

| *Year* | *Area under Mulberry (Hectares)* | *DFLs (lakh Nos.)* | *Reeling Cocoons (tonnes)* | *Raw Silk (tonnes)* | *Silk Waste (tonnes)* |
|---|---|---|---|---|---|
| 1980–81 | 1,70,000 | 2,189.51 | 58,208 | 4,593 | 1,376 |
| 1981–82 | 1,79,949 | 2,420.66 | 55,210 | 4,801 | 1,523 |
| 1982–83 | 1,96,848 | 2,520.00 | 66,811 | 5,214 | 1,825 |
| 1983–84 | 2,06,913 | 2,699.51 | 71,276 | 5,681 | 2,071 |
| 1984–85 | 2,14,838 | 2,572.01 | 74,875 | 6,895 | 2,464 |
| 1985–86 | 2,17,839 | 2,628.79 | 76,717 | 7,029 | 2,504 |
| 1986–87 | 2,29,758 | 2,767.68 | 81,573 | 7,905 | 2,837 |
| 1987–88 | 2,41,603 | 3,007.77 | 86,528 | 8,455 | 3,086 |
| 1988–89 | 2,68,063 | 3,008.95 | 96,471 | 9,683 | 3,399 |
| 1989–90 | 2,94,241 | 3,478.68 | 1,10,433 | 10,905 | 3,921 |
| 1990–91 | 3,13,109 | 3,170.30 | 1,16,672 | 11,487 | 3,953 |

*Source* : C.S.B. Silk in India, Statistical Biennial, 1992, Bangalore, p. 57.

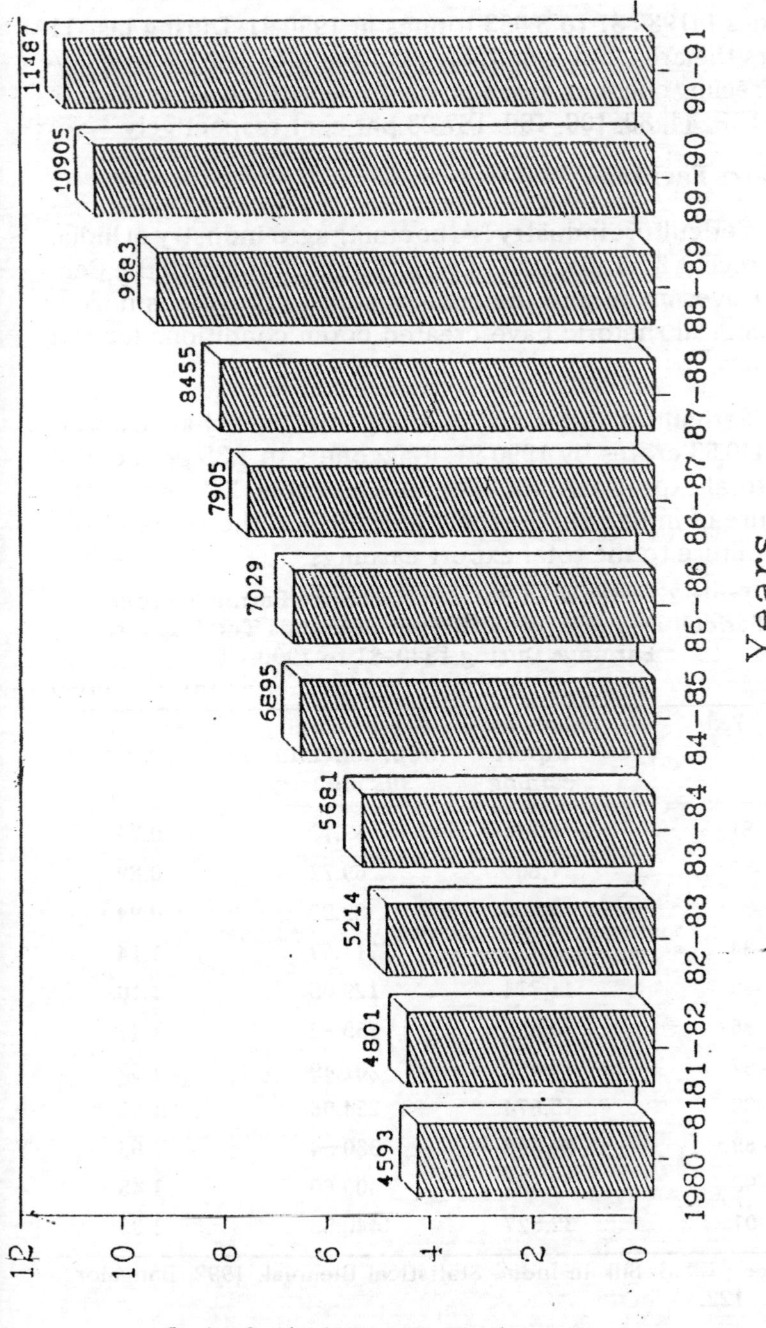


**Fig. 2.1 : Raw Silk Production in India (in thousand tonnes)**

tonnes in1980-81 to 3,953 tonnes in 1990-91. During last 11 years the area under mulberry cultivation, disease free laying, reeling cocoons, raw silk, waste, registered a growth rate of 84.18, 44, 80, 100, 150. 187.28 per cent respectively.

## Export Earnings

Sericulture industry is a booming agro-industry of India. The recent liberalisation of export-import policy of the Central Government and the general shift to pragmatism from ideological rhetoric have created boom conditions for silk exports.[7]

Sericulture industry is earning foreign exchange about Rs. 440.53 crores by 1990-91. It accounts to 1.35 per cent of the total export earning of India. The Table 2.3 reveals the picture of India's total export earning and the share of the sericulture to the total export earnings.

**Table 2.3 : Share of Foreign Exchange Earnings From Sericulture Industry With That of India's Total Export Earnings During 1980–81 to 1990–91**

*(Rs. in crores)*

| *Year* | *India's total export earning* | *Export earnings from sericulture/ silk industry* | *Percentage to total* |
|---|---|---|---|
| 1980–81 | 6,711 | 53.12 | 0.79 |
| 1981–82 | 7,806 | 69.73 | 0.89 |
| 1982–83 | 8,803 | 82.85 | 0.94 |
| 1983–84 | 9,771 | 111.67 | 1.14 |
| 1984–85 | 11,774 | 129.05 | 1.10 |
| 1985–86 | 10,895 | 159.82 | 1.47 |
| 1986–87 | 12,452 | 201.49 | 1.62 |
| 1987–88 | 15,674 | 254.96 | 1.63 |
| 1988–89 | 20,302 | 330.54 | 1.63 |
| 1989–90 | 27,681 | 400.60 | 1.45 |
| 1990–91 | 32,527 | 440.53 | 1.35 |

*Source* : C.S.B. Silk in India, Statistical Biennial, 1992, Bangalore, p. 122.

## Sericulture as a Means of Income Levelling

Sericulture plays a vital role in transferring wealth from richer sections to poorer sections of the society. Silk is consumed mostly by the affluent and the money so spent by them on purchase of silk is distributed among the sericulturists, reelers, weavers and traders.

Summary of the percentage distribution of money from sale of soft silk fabrics of weight 40,50 and 60 gms/mtr is given in Table 2.4 which has also shown in Figure 2.2

It is clear from the table that a major portion of the income (51.5 per cent) from the sale of one metre of 40 gm. weight silk cloth goes to the cocoon producer. The reeler, twister, weaver and trader receives 6.2, 8.2 14.5 and 19.5 respectively. The share of cocoon producer increases to 60 gms. per metre.

Hence, it can be concluded that, the (gross) income received by the primary farmer from the sales of any agro-based product tends to be minimal and often less than others who handle the produce before it finally reaches the end user in the case of silk, the primary sericulturist who grows the

**Table 2.4 : Percentage Distribution of Money**

*(sale proceeds) (% share)*

| *Category of Persons* | *Soft silk fabric of* 40 Gms/mtr. | *50 Gms,/mtr.* | *60 Gms./mtr.* |
|---|---|---|---|
| Cocoon producer | 51.5 | 54.6 | 56.8 |
| Reeler | 6.2 | 6.6 | 6.8 |
| Twister | 8.2 | 8.7 | 9.1 |
| Weaver | 14.5 | 12.3 | 10.7 |
| Trader | 19.5 | 17.8 | 16.6 |
| **Total** | **100.00** | **100.00** | **100.00** |

*Source* : C.S.B. Silk in India, Statistical Biennial, 1992, Bangalore, p. 122.

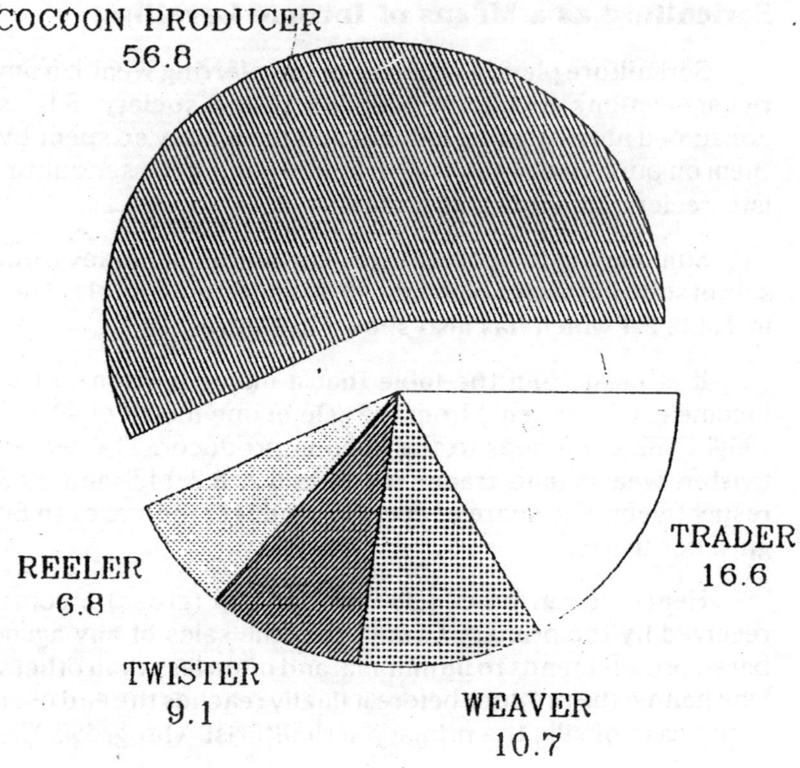


**Fig. 2.2 : Distribution of Gross Income From Sale of Soft Silk Fabrics of 60 gms./mtr.**

food plant, raises the silkworm and sells the cocoons gets the maximum income from the sale proceeds.

## Employment

Out of the 5,76,000 villages in India, sericulture is practised in about 50,000 villages providing employment to about six million persons, most of them belonged to the weaker sections of the society.[8] During 1981-82, the persons employed in sericulture industry were only 44.55 lakhs. Now the number has increased from 44.55 to 65.00 by 1990-91, it shows the growth rate of 46 per cent.

The Table No. 2.5 shows the trends in employment in sericulture industry.

**Table 2.5 : Employment in Sericulture Industry in India**

*(in lakhs)*

| *Year* | *Persons Employed* |
|---|---|
| 1981–82 | 44.55 |
| 1982–83 | 46.00 |
| 1983–84 | 50.50 |
| 1984–85 | 51.52 |
| 1985–86 | 53.64 |
| 1986–87 | 55.00 |
| 1987–88 | 57.65 |
| 1988–89 | 60.30 |
| 1989–90 | N.B. |
| 1990–91 | 65.00* |

*Note*: * Projected figure. C.S.B. Silk in India, Statistical Biennial, 1992, Bangalore, p. 15.

*Source* : C.S.B. Silk in India, Statistical Biennial, 1988, Bangalore, p. 73.

## Family Labour

The involvement of family labour under both irrigated and mulberry cultivation is about 46 per cent and remain is hired labour. The utilisation of family labour generally reduces the total cost of production to some extent. In the Rayalaseema districts of Andhra Pradesh, the participation of family labour in mulberry cultivation and silkworm rearing accounts for 68 per cent.[9]

In India women constitute about 48.7 per cent of the total population. If the rural poverty has to be eradicated and the rural households are to be made economically viable, rural women should be given suitable employment. Sericulture is a promising appropriate technology which can generate employment for rural women. An acre of mulberry could provide gainful employment for five persons. Many of the landless labourers could also gain employment through silk production. Sericulture meets the national objectives of providing employment opportunities to tribals, villages and women and could help containing migration from villages to towns and cities.[10]

## Creation of Promotional Agencies

The role of sericulture in engaging abundant manpower with gainful employment is very significant. But whatever the activity may be, it shall not come up without proper support and financial assistance from the government. Moreover in the post-independence era, mulberry sericulture was characterised by low productivity both in terms of leaf yield as well as the quality of cocoons. The conditions of non-mulberry sericulture was even worse at it was confined to the hilly areas. The Government of India set up silk development directorate in 1945. A silk panel was also established to suggest measures for sericulture development. This silk panel suggested a 15 year prospective plan for the development of sericulture and recommended for the establishment of Central Silk Board for ensuring the coordinated development of industry under Central control.

## Central Silk Board

Central Silk Board is a statutory body under the administrative control of the Ministry of Textiles, Government of India. One of the earliest commodity boards constituted in April, 1949 under an act of the Parliament (Act No. LXI of 1948).[11] The Central Silk Board is entrusted with the overall responsibility of developing silk industry covering the full gamut of sericultural activities in the country. It is an organisation, triennially constituted with 36 members, including the Chairman and representatives drawn from both Houses of Parliament, sericulture states and special interests representing both industry and trade.

## Organisational Set-up

The Board's term is three years and it has 36 members, including the Chairman, Vice-Chairman, Member Secretary,

Representative of the Lok Sabha and the Rajya Sabha, nominees of the Central and State Governments and Representatives from among rearers, reelers, the trade and industry. The Central Silk Board has been entrusted with the overall objective of developing the silk industry. The main functions of the Central Silk Board as envisaged in the Act are:

- Promotion and development of silk industry, by such measures as it thinks fit.
- Undertaking, assisting and encouraging scientific, technological and economic research.
- Developing and distributing healthy silkworm feeds.
- Devising means for improved method of mulberry cultivation, silkworm rearing, silk reeling and spinning.
- Initiating measures of standardisation and quality of control of silk and silk products.
- Rationalisation of marketing and stabilisation of prices of silk cocoons and raw silk.
- Organising pre-shipment inspection of silk products for export.
- Collection of statistics.
- Preparing and furnishing relevant reports relating to silk industry.
- Advising the Central Government on all matters relating to the development of silk industry, including the import of raw silk and export of silk products.

## Central Sericulture Research and Training

Initial efforts in the fifties of transplanting temperate technologies failed and the need for tropical-oriented research in sericulture was realised. For this purpose the Central Sericulture Research and Training Institute (CSRTI) was established in Mysore in 1962 and the station at Berhampur was reorganised. During the last 25 years the research institute has been able to evolve several high yielding mulberry varieties utilising the local and exotic races. Mention may be made of S50, S30, S36 and S41. The Kanva-2, a selected mulberry variety, is now very popular with the sericulturists in South India. The package of practices prescribed by this institute after sustained efforts have helped in the doubling in per unit mulberry leaf yield.

The new technology of silkworm rearing suitable to the tropical conditions was developed in 70s by the institute. This helped in stabilising the cocoon crops, spread of sericulture industry in non-traditional areas and introduction of high yielding silkworm races. An integrated approach has been developed to control grassier and muscardine disease of silkworm namely 'Resham keet oushadh'. To prevent Uzy fly infestation, a product namely uzicide has been developed. These two are very popular among sericulturists.

## National Sericulture Project

The biggest impetus in recent times to the development of Indian sericulture was provided by the commencement of Rs. 555 crore National Sericulture Project (NSP) conceived by the Central Silk Board for development of mulberry sericulture, and assisted by the World Bank and the Swiss Development Cooperation. The project is under implementation from 1989, in 17 major States of India. In the traditional sericulture States of Karnataka, Tamil Nadu, Andhra Pradesh, West Bengal and Jammu and Kashmir, the project is implemented by the Department of Sericulture.

## Broad objectives of National Sericulture Project

(a) Introduction of sericulture in new States, and in areas of sericultural states and expansion of area under mulberry by 58,000 hectares by the end of 1994.

(b) Increasing the raw milk production in the country by an additional 6,000 tonnes by 1994, including 1,000 tonnes of superior bivoltine silk.

(c) Improving the quality and productivity of Indian silk, by the introduction of specific measures.

(d) Generating employment opportunities in rural areas for an additional one million people, a majority of whom belonging to economically weaker sections.

(e) Increasing the quantum of Indian silk product exports by an additional Rs. 57,000 millions by 1994.

(f) Strengthening the infrastructure for research, extension, seed production, silk processing, implementation of measures for quality control in the silk production system and development of market support for cocoons as well as raw silk.

(q) Providing financial support to rearers, reelers, twisters and seed producers through Commercial Banks, and through the provisions under the component of working capital assistance to reelers of the National Sericulture Project.

(h) Promoting increased participation of private sector in silkworm seed production, supply of chawkie and reeling.

(i) Strengthening socially desirable features such as development of women, promotion of smokeless chulhas in reeling establishments, improvement of water conservation and rainfed technology and improvement of non-governmental organisations for promotion of sericulture.

## Progress Through Five Year Plans

With the advent of economic planning in the country sericulture industry made progressive development through the consecutive plans (vide Table 2.6)

Sericulture did not find a separate place in First Five Year Plan, which was included under the "other village industries". Central assistance was made available to the States by the Board as grants and loans for implementation of specific approved schemes. During the plan period, a total amount of Rs. 45.97 lakh was made available to the States, out of which Rs. 21.69 lakh was utilised. The percentage of utilisation was low due to paucity of trained personnel and delay in constructional activities.

Out of an allocation of Rs. 379.25 lakhs for implementation of 339 schemes, about Rs. 224.49 lakhs representing nearly 60 per cent of the provision was utilised by the States. In the Central sector, the outlay was Rs. 35.17 lakhs and the expenditure was Rs. 26.13 lakhs. The production of raw silk increased from 14.86 lakh kg. to 15.13 lakhs kg.

The total amount allocated during Second Five Year Plan under both Central and State projects was Rs. 414.42 lakhs. But the amount sanctioned was Rs. 307.53 lakhs and the expenditure reported was only Rs. 250.62 lakhs. From this it is clear that adequate attention was not shown towards sericulture development during the early period of planning in India.

An outlay of Rs. 702.01 lakhs was approved for the development of the industry during the Third Plan period of which Rs. 552.01 lakhs related to State schemes and Rs. 150.00 lakhs for Central schemes to the implemented through the Central Silk Board. The total expenditure incurred by the States was Rs. 339.42 accounting for Rs. 62.6 of the allocation, an expenditure of Rs. 72.32 lakhs was incurred in the respect of Central schemes.

The total amount allocated during the Third Five Year Plan under both Central and States project was Rs. 702.01 lakhs. But the amount sanctioned Rs. 548.01 lakhs and expenditure reported only Rs. 411.74 lakhs. From this it is clear that Rs. 136.27 lakhs was left unutilised.

During the Fourth Plan Period, the allocation to States and Central projects was Rs. 969 lakhs. Utilisation was Rs.

674.99, it is clear that under this plan period, sericulture industry did not get momentum.

After the inception of drought-prone area programme during the Fifth Five Year Plan sericulture gained momentum. An amount of Rs. 16,737 lakhs was allotted during the Sixth Five Year Plan under both Central and State projects and out of which Rs. 12,637.67 lakhs was utilised. Thus, the expenditure on sericulture has shown a rapid increase from Rs. 250.62 lakhs during the second five year plan, which signifies the attention drawn towards the development of sericulture.

During the Seventh Plan period, the allocation to the States and Central project was Rs. 31.078 lakhs and out of which an amount of Rs. 29,404.63 was utilised. From this, it is clear that the allotment and expenditure on sericulture are moving in an approximate ratio. By the end of the plan period production of raw silk reached the level of 120.16 tonnes and silk export earnings amounted to Rs. 400.61 crore.

## Eight Five Year Plan (1992-1997)

The Government under the Planning Commission had constituted a sub-group on sericulture for formulation of sericulture development programmes for Eight Plan. The final outlay for development of sericulture during Eight Plan both under Central and State sector was Rs. 860.76 crores as per the details given below.

| | |
|---|---|
| 1. Allocation under State's plan programmes, including the two years provision of National Sericulture project for five States. | Rs. 583.55 Crores |
| 2. Central sector provision of developmental programmes to be implemented by Central Silk Board, including two years provision for CSB component of National Sericulture Project. | Rs. 277.21 Crores |
| **Total.** | **Rs. 860.76 Crores** |

**Table 2.6 : Financial Allocation to Sericulture during Plan Periods**

*(Rs. in Crores)*

| Sl. No. | Period | Central Project | | State Project | | Amount sanctioned | Expenditure reported |
|---|---|---|---|---|---|---|---|
| | | Allocation | Amount sanctioned | Expenditure | Allocation | | |
| 1. | Second Plan (1956–61) | 35.17 | 38.80 | 26.13 | 379.25 | 268.73 | 224.49 |
| 2. | Third Plan (1961–66) | 150.00 | 76.58 | 72.32 | 552.01 | 471.43 | 339.42 |
| 3. | Transitional period (1966–69) | 70.24 | 71.04 | 62.32 | 442.28 | 307.63 | 218.98 |
| 4. | Fourth Plan (1969–74) | 130.00 | 99.56 | 81.61 | 839.00 | 763.40 | 593.38 |
| 5. | Fifth Plan (1974–78) | 861.20 | 788.00 | 526.17 | 1,693.18 | — | 1,109.06 |
| 6. | Transitional period (1978–80) | 1,320.00 | — | 110.46 | 1,589.71 | — | 1,259.26 |
| 7. | Sixth Plan (1980–85) | 3,100.00 | 4,000.00 | 3,715.00 | 13,635.00 | — | 8,922.67 |
| 8. | Seventh Plan (1985–90) | 7,000.00 | — | 8,816.00 | 24,078.00 | 25,299.69 | 20,588.89 |
| | Total | 12,566.61 | 5,068.98 | 13,470.01 | 43,250.43 | 27,110.88 | 33,255.89 |

*Source* : C.S.B. Statistical Biennial, 1992, Bangalore, p. 12.

The sub-group has also suggested the following targets of production, exports and employment for the Eighth Plan.

| | |
|---|---|
| 1. Area expansion (Hectares) | |
| Mulberry | |
| i) Irrigated | 3,00,000 |
| ii) Rainfed | 1,25,000 |
| **Total** | **4,25,000** |
| 2. Raw Silk production (tonnes) | |
| a) Mulberry | |
| i) Multi X Bivoltine | 18,000 |
| ii) Bivoltine | 2,000 |
| **Sub-total** | **20,000** |
| b) Non-mulberry | |
| i) Tropical tasar | 600 |
| ii) Oak Tasar | 50 |
| iii) Eri | 650 |
| iv) Muga | 100 |
| **Sub-total** | **1,400** |
| **Grand Total** | **21,400** |
| 3. Employment generation | 65 lakh persons (Cumulative) |
| 4. Export | 3.074 crores |

Source : C.S.B. Statistical Biennial, 1992, Bangalore, p. 15.

The Table No. 2.7 explains the State-wise production of mulberry raw silk for the year 1990-91. The concentration of villages for sericulture production among various States in India, Karnataka is the highest i.e., 16,593 villages and the lowest is Sikkim i.e., six villages. Here, it is mentioned that Goa and Haryana States are not cultivated sericultural crops due to climatic conditions.

**Table 2.7 : State-wise Production of Mulberry Raw Silk Production 1990–91**

| *Sl. No.* | *State* | *No. of Sericulture Villages* | *Production of mulberry raw silk (in tonnes)* |
|---|---|---|---|
| 1. | Andhra Pradesh | 9,377 | 3,194 * |
| 2. | Assam | 7,102 | 18 |
| 3. | Arunachal Pradesh | 100 | 1 |
| 4. | Bihar | 4,777 | 65 |
| 5. | Gujarat | 137 | neg |
| 6. | Himachal Pradesh | 1,687 | 8 |
| 7. | Jammu and Kashmir | 2,620 | 18 |
| 8. | Karnataka | 16,593 | 6,214 |
| 9. | Kerala | N.A. | 1 |
| 10. | Madhya Pradesh | 1,314 | 9 |
| 11. | Maharashtra | 1,357 | 6 |
| 12. | Manipur | 354 | 23 |
| 13. | Mizoram | 60 | neg |
| 14. | Meghalaya | 1,812 | 1 |
| 15. | Nagaland | 140 | 1 |
| 16. | Orissa | 2,300 | 3 |
| 17. | Punjab | 818 | neg |
| 18. | Rajasthan | 114 | 1 |
| 19. | Sikkim | 6 | — |
| 20. | Tamil Nadu | 4,985 | 1,072 * |
| 21. | Tripura | 278 | 2 |
| 22. | Uttar Pradesh | 2,017 | 21 |
| 23. | West Bengal | 1,580 | 829 |
| | Total | | 11,487 |

*Note* : * estimated. Neg : Negligible

*Source* : C.S.B. Statistical Biennial, Bangalore, p. 73.

The Table also explains about the production of mulberry raw silk in various States of India. Karnataka is the largest producer of mulberry raw silk, accounting for 6,214 tonnes. That means, about 54 per cent of total mulberry raw silk produced in the country and it is followed by Andhra Pradesh State which accounts for 3,194 tonnes i.e., 28 per cent. Only one tonne of mulberry raw silk produced by the five States viz., Arunachal Pradesh, Kerala, Meghalaya, Nagaland and Rajasthan for the year 1990-91.

Only three States viz., Gujarat, Mizoram and Punjab are producing mulberry raw silk below 0.50 tonne (negligible). It may be concluded that Karnataka, Andhra Pradesh and Tamil Nadu States are producing higher quantum of mulberry raw silk.

## Sericulture in Andhra Pradesh

Andhra Pradesh is the fifth largest State both in area and population. It is known as river State and rice bowl of South India. It is now having 23 districts distributed among the three well-known regions of the State—four districts in Rayalaseema, nine districts in Coastal Andhra and 10 districts in Telangana. Sericulture is ideally suited to a predominantly agricultural State like Andhra Pradesh. The main concentration has been in the Rayalaseema region of the state, where climatic conditions are favourable for this industry, Andhra Pradesh produce both mulberry and tasar silk.

Andhra Pradesh achieved significant place in the development of sericulture, although it has no place in the sericulture map of India in 1956 when the State was formed with the integration of Telangana with the then Andhra Pradesh. In the year 1953, the area under mulberry cultivation in Andhra State was just 5 acres. It reached to 40 acres when Andhra Pradesh was formed in 1956. It means that Andhra Pradesh was not a traditional sericulture State. It is a new entrant into this sericulture enterprise.

For a long time, Palamaneru in Chittoor district had sericulture farm in composite Madras State. Because of the efforts of Sri S.V. Ramamurthy, adviser to the Governor of Madras province, sericulture spread to the areas of Hindupur, Araku and other places. Sericulture was practised in a small way with the setting up of a few farms by the Government at Lepakshi, Bhadrachalam, Chintalapalli, Chintalapudi and Palamaneru after 1970-71. Keeping in view the importance and potential for the development of sericulture in the State a separate department was established by the State Government in 1981.[12]

## Area Under Mulberry Cultivation

The area under mulberry cultivation in Andhra Pradesh increased from 635 acres in 1970-71 to 48,674 acres in 1980-81 and further to 1,88,580 acres during 1990-91. Mulberry sericulture has become an established industry in the area adjoining to Karnataka plateau especially in the districts of Anantapur and Chittoor. Out of 23 districts in Andhra Pradesh almost all districts are practising mulberry sericulture. The Table No. 2.8 shows the district-wise distribution of hectarage under mulberry cultivation.

The Table 2.8 makes the clear that 85 per cent of the total mulberry hectarage is concentrated in the four districts of Rayalaseema namely Anantapur, Chittoor, Kurnool, Cuddapah. Among these four districts of Rayalaseema, Anantapur district ranks first with 26,868 hectares of area under mulberry cultivation.

## Infrastructure

Sericulture in Andhra Pradesh attained momentum only after 1970 as government created the necessary infrastructure facilities for the sericulture development.[13]

The Table No. 2.9 makes it clear that, the government has been creating adequate facilities in order to encourage mulberry cultivation and raring of cocoons in Andhra Pradesh.

**Table 2.8 : District-wise Distribution of Area Under Mulberry Cultivation in Andhra Pradesh During 1988–89**

| *Sl. No.* | *Districts* | *Area under Mulberry* | |
|---|---|---|---|
| | | *In Hectares* | *Percentage* |
| 1. | Anantapur | 26,868 | 47.90 |
| 2. | Chittoor | 9,202 | 16.49 |
| 3. | Cuddapah | 6,456 | 11.52 |
| 4. | Kurnool | 4,814 | 8.59 |
| 5. | Prakasam | 945 | 1.68 |
| 6. | Nellore | 357 | 0.63 |
| 7. | Guntur | 471 | 0.84 |
| 8. | Krishna | 601 | 1.07 |
| 9. | East Godavari | 736 | 1.39 |
| 10. | West Godavari | 605 | 1.08 |
| 11. | Visakhapatnam | 578 | 1.04 |
| 12. | Vijayanagaram | 524 | 0.94 |
| 13. | Srikakulam | 323 | 0.57 |
| 14. | Mahaboobnagar | 366 | 0.65 |
| 15. | Rangareddy | 338 | 0.60 |
| 16. | Nalgonda | 144 | 0.25 |
| 17. | Karimnagar | 770 | 1.37 |
| 18. | Nizamabad | 78 | 0.13 |
| 19. | Adilabad | 284 | 0.50 |
| 20. | Warangal | 221 | 0.93 |
| 21. | Khammam | 577 | 1.03 |
| 22. | Medak | 440 | 0.78 |
| 23. | Hyderabad | — | — |
| | Total | 55,998 | 100.00 |

*Source* : Department of Sericulture, Anantapur.

The Department of Sericulture has paid special attention to overcome most of the problems in rearing of cocoons and silk reeling.

**Table 2.9 : Infrastructure Facilities to Sericulture in Andhra Pradesh 1990–92**

| Sl. No. | Item | Number |
|---|---|---|
| 1. | Government Grainages | 42 |
| 2. | Private grainages | 34 |
| 3. | Government cocoon markets | 11 |
| 4. | Co-operative socieiteis | 130 |
| 5. | Government farms/seed farms/ demonstration farms | 50 |
| 6. | Silk reeling units under State deptt. | 41 |
| 7. | Government chawkie rearing centres | 32 |
| 8. | Tasar cocoon markets | 9 |

*Source* : Deputy Director, Department of Sericulture, Anantpaur.

## Incentives Offered by the Government

To develop the silk industry, the Andhra Pradesh Government is giving the following incentives to the sericulturists :

(1) Free mulberry cutting up to Rs. 250 per 0.40 hectares (per acre) for local procurement and Rs. 400 for outside State procurement are being supplied in the areas of Rayalaseema.

(2) Under Integrated Rural Development Programme (IRDP) subsidy at the rate of 33 1/3 per cent and 25 per cent is being given to marginal and small farmers respectively at the unit cost of Rs. 10,500 per 0.40 hectares (per acre).

(3) 50 per cent subsidy is being given for supply of Uzy fly nylon nets (50 per cent from States and 50 per cent from Central funds).

(4) Rs. 5 per kg. is being given on production of bivoltgine cocoons ( 50 per cent from State and 50 per cent from Central Government).

(5) Premium for crop insurance is being subsidised by 50 per cent for local race seed rearers and,

(6) In the year 1989 government has agreed to give :

(a) Rs. 5 per kg. as price support to tribals to the production of mulberry reeling cocoons.

(b) 50 per cent subsidy on rearing equipment.

(c) 100 per cent subsidy on premium for crop insurance to bivoltine rearers.

(d) Full subsidy on premium for crop tasar crop.

(e) Rs. 15 per kg. on excess production of local raw seed cocoons to seed rearers.[14]

Each Scheduled Caste beneficiary is provided with a free rearing shed worth of Rs. 5,000 each and Rs. 3,000 for equipment on loan basis and Rs. 1,000 loan for cultivation. High yielding variety of mulberry cuttings are supplied freely. Each Scheduled Tribe beneficiary is provided with 50 per cent subsidy and 20 per cent margin money in the unit cost of Rs. 10,500. The balance 30 per cent amount is the loan composition.

**Financial Assistance**

During the Seventh Plan period, the Government of Andhra Pradesh has taken up master programme for the development of sericulture in the State. It also laid more emphasis on other plans and projects which lead towards growth of sericulture. It is proposed to bring an additional area of 10,117 hectares under mulberry cultivation to increase silkworm egg production to meet the demand to increase the production of mulberry reeling cocoons from 15,000 tonnes to 30,000 tonnes and set up P1 seed farms technical service centres to encourage production of silk. The Planning Commission has sanctioned Rs. 240.78 crores for the development of sericulture in different states out of which Rs. 26.70 crores is allotted to Andhra Pradesh.[15]

Funds are liberally allotted for the development of sericulture in the State under DPAP. Within a short period of 10 years, Andhra Pradesh achieved second place among silk producing States in the country.

An interesting feature of Andhra Pradesh regarding sericulture development is that the State has utilised all the programmes announced by the Central Government to a maximum extent and benefited. From 1980-81 onwards the State is getting financial assistance under IRDP, Special Employment Scheme, Rehabilitation, Inter-State Tasar Project, Special Central Assistance for Scheduled Caste Tribal Action Plan, Social Foresty, Integrated Tribal Development Agency, Water Shed Area Programme, Drought Releif Works and Indo-Swiss Assistance Programme besides plan allocation.[16] Though a detailed picture of the additional resources utilised is not available, the Table No. 2.10 throws light on the nature of resources made available to the sericulture during 1988-89.

**Table 2.10 : Particulars of Resources Allocation for Sericulture Development in Andhra Pradesh (1988–89)**

*(Rs. in Lakhs)*

| *Sl. No.* | *Plan/Project* | *Outlay* | *Expenditure* |
|---|---|---|---|
| 1. | Non-plan | 279.977 | 254.006 |
| 2. | Plan 400.00 | 381.119 | |
| 3. | DPAP127.435 | 99.965 | |
| 4. | IRDP | | |
| | a) Infrastructure | 35.830 | 20.040 |
| | b) Loaning Programme | 173.810 | 146.940 |
| 5. | Special Central Assistance | | |
| | a) Loan | 72.840 | 85.000 (a + b) |
| | b) Grant | 105.618 | |
| | c) Subsidies | 64.640 | 57.780 |
| 6. | ITDA212.970 | 115.000 | |
| 7. | Social Foresty | 21.980 | 17.000 |
| 8. | Indo-Swiss Programme | 29.992 | 50.807 |
| | Total1,525.092 | 1,227.657 | |

*Source* : Office of the Deputy Director, Department of Sericulture, Anantapur.

**Swiss Aid**

The mulberry sericulture development programme is being implemented in Andhra Pradesh and Tamil Nadu States with the help of Switzerland Government. It involves a total outlay of Rs. 3.05 crores for the period from 1987-88 to 1989-90 for both the States. The share of Swiss aid to Andhra Pradesh is Rs. 131.05 lakhs and the share of Andhra Pradesh Government is Rs. 10.08 lakhs. The total outlay of the project is Rs. 141.13 lakhs.[17] The main objective of implementing the project is to improve the status of small and marginal farmers engaged in sericulture cultivation.

The programme includes the construction of (1) chawki rearing centres (2) infrastructure facilities for silk reeling (3) mobile disinfection units and (4) providing training to silk reelers. In addition to the above, it also includes providing facilities for marketing cocoons, and production of bivoltine yarn.

**World Bank Assistance**

The World Bank has sanctioned Rs. 940.264 lakhs for the development of sericulture in the State in the year 1990-91. This amount is distributed among 20 districts in the State through National Bank for Agriculture and Rural Development (NABARD).

The World Bank aid is meant for development of sericulture for purchasing pumpsets, digging of borewells, purchase of seeds, fertilisers, modern agricultural implements and for the construction of rearing house. Under this programme an amount of Rs. 860.264 lakhs is proposed for farm practices and the remaining Rs. 80 lakhs for non-farm operations. Anantapur, Chittoor district are given top priority in this looming programmes. The Table No. 2.11 indicates the district-wise distribution of loan amounts and subsidies by the World Bank in Andhra Pradesh for the year 1990-91.

It is evident from the Table 2.11 that the loan and subsidy extended by the World Bank is adequate to meet the require-

**Table 2.11 : Details of the Loans and Subsidies given to Sericulture by the World Bank 1990–91**

*(Rs. in Lakhs)*

| Sl. No. | Districts | Loans | Subsidy | District Funds | Total |
|---|---|---|---|---|---|
| 1. | Anantapur | 184.66 | 15.61 | 16.51 | 246.79 |
| 2. | Chittoor | 127.97 | 34.37 | 8.78 | 171.13 |
| 3. | Kurnool | 68.96 | 20.03 | 2.87 | 94.81 |
| 4. | Cuddapah | 71.89 | 20.03 | 2.87 | 94.81 |
| 5. | Prakasam | 22.31 | 5.42 | 0.83 | 28.57 |
| 6. | Nellore | 16.61 | 3.62 | 0.83 | 21.07 |
| 7. | Guntur | 16.61 | 3.62 | 0.83 | 21.07 |
| 8. | Krishna | 16.14 | 4.65 | 0.20 | 20.49 |
| 9. | West Godavari | 16.51 | 4.70 | 0.27 | 21.49 |
| 10. | East Godavari | 16.98 | 5.16 | 0.17 | 22.33 |
| 11. | Visakhapatnam | 22.09 | 6.74 | 0.30 | 29.14 |
| 12. | Mahaboobnagar | 22.51 | 6.27 | 0.35 | 29.14 |
| 13. | Rangareddy | 11.92 | 3.65 | 0.16 | 17.74 |
| 14. | Nalgonda | 04.34 | 1.19 | 0.09 | 5.61 |
| 15. | Medak | 06.86 | 1.65 | 0.18 | 8.70 |
| 16. | Nizamabad | 02.69 | 0.76 | 0.05 | 3.45 |
| 17. | Karimnagar | 27.01 | 8.00 | 0.35 | 35.37 |
| 18. | Warangal | 01.34 | 1.19 | 0.09 | 5.64 |
| 19. | Khammam | 05.51 | 1.60 | 0.15 | 7.30 |
| 20. | Adilabad | 11.59 | 3.18 | 0.24 | 15.02 |
| | Total | 713.16 | 191.09 | 36.01 | 940.26 |

Source : Office of the Joint Director, Department of Sericulture, Anantapur.

ments of sericulturists in different districts. The estimated number of beneficiaries are 7,284 in the 20 districts of Andhra Pradesh. Out of the total assistance of Rs. 940 lakhs, loan portion is Rs. 713.16 lakhs and subsidy amount accounts to Rs. 191.09 lakhs besides own funds of districts to the extent of Rs. 36.01 lakhs. Out of the total number of 7,284 units, Anantapur district is given first preference for receiving financial assistance followed by Chittoor, Kurnool, Cuddapah districts. The main objective of this World Bank project is to increase the present production of 1,000 tonnes of silk yarn to 2,500 tonnes per annum. To achieve this target, an additional area of 10,000 hectares of land has to be brought under mulberry cultivation. The total cost of the project is estimated at Rs. 104,998 crores. This includes the institutional finance of Rs. 57.624 crores. The World Bank has given its content to share of Rs. 118.44 crores development of sericulture in Andhra Pradesh. It is estimated that this project would create employment opportunities to 1.25 lakh people.[18]

## Progress of Sericulture in Rayalaseema Districts

Climatic conditions prevailing in Anantapur and Chittoor are more favourable for the development of mulberry cultivation and silkworm rearing. The other factor that governs the concentration of sericulture in these districts is severe drought condition. While other agricultural crops wither away, mulberry crop survives and yields atleast two successful crops out of five crops. In addition to the above factor, one more factor is the availability of financial assistance from Central and State Governments with a view to improve the drought areas and to benefit small and marginal farmers in the above districts.

During 1988-89, the total raw silk product in Andhra Pradesh was 29,889.10 kg., out of which 20,741.33 kg. of raw silk was produced only in four Rayalaseema districts as given in the Table No. 2.12. It accounts to 69.4 per cent of the total raw silk produced in the State by providing employment to a considerable extent.

The progress of sericulture in the four districts of Rayalaseema is presented in the following analysis. Though the region is known for frequent droughts and famines, it is rich in terms of the development of sericulture.

**Table 2.12 : Raw Silk Production in Rayalaseema Districts, 1988–89**

| *Sl. No.* | *District* | *Raw Silk Production (in kg.)* |
|---|---|---|
| 1. | Anantapur | 9,838.59 |
| 2. | Chittoor | 7,054.60 |
| 3. | Cuddapah | 1,708.11 |
| 4. | Kurnool | 2,140.03 |
| | **Total** | **20,741.33** |

Source : Office of the Deputy Director, Department of Sericulture, Anantapur

## Chittoor District

Chittoor district ranks second in cocoon production in Andhra Pradesh. In this district, farmers adopted Kanva-2 or M5 variety of mulberry cultivation which has increased the area from 2,290.5 hectares in 1979-80 to 9,214.18 hectares in 1988-89 from the inception of DPAP.[19] About Rs.226.63 lakhs had been allocated for the development of sericulture in the district by the government. The raw silk production has also increased from 8.30 lakhs kg. in 1980-81 to 63.020 lakhs in 1988-89. The district produced 238 lakhs bivoltine cocoons during 1988-89. A subsidy to the extent of Rs. 136.91 lakhs had been provided to 6,196 small and marginal farmers for sericulture development.[20]

A silkworm seed unit was established at Horsely Hills in 1980-81 with the help of District Rural Development Agency (DRDA). This unit located at an altitude of 1,424 m. above MSL was started for the purpose of supplying cross breed layings for the farmers in different districts. For this purpose this unit obtained P3 silkworm seed from the breeds stock of CSRTI, Mysore and after rearing the required quantity of P2 seed is produced and supplied to the seed farms in the State.[21] This unit is established at the cost of Rs. 11 lakhs has produced about 1.44 lakhs pure Mysore and 70,000 bivoltine variety and supplied to several and stations.

An Indo-Japanese vanture for the production of bivoltine and multivoltine eggs has been started at Ramasamudram in Punganur taluk. The capacity of this unit is about 1.20 lakhs boxes per annum. This project is first of its kind in the country started producing in 1989. This project, which costs Rs. 3 crore will enable different states, including Andhra Pradesh, to switch on to bivoltine sericulture wherever it is feasible for the production of high quality silk.[22]

## Cuddapah District

Cuddapah district too has made rapid strides in the sericulture devlopment with the financial assistance provided by DPAP. The area under mulberry cultivation has increased from 28.32 hectares (1976-77) to 6,457 hectares in 1988-89. The industry covers about 11,000 small and marginal farmers. Rayachoti, Lakkireddipalli and Rajampet are some of the places where sericulture has some progress in this district.

The infrastructure facilities created includes four seed farms, two grainages, three silkworm rearing units, three silk reeling units, one cocoon market and one silk twisting unit. The silkworm egg production has increased from 2.30 lakhs in 1980-81 to 17.20 lakhs in 1988–89, while cocoon production rose from 0.80 lakhs kg. to 20,430 lakhs kg. during the same period. A subsidy of Rs. 4 lakhs was given to the farmers for the development of sericulture in the district.[23]

## Kurnool District

An amount of Rs. 267 lakhs had been released since 1978-79 for the development of sericulture in Kurnool district. The production of eggs has increased from 0.80 lakhs in 1978-79 to 16.12 lakhs by the end of 1988-89. Mulberry cultivation also increased from 28.32 hectares to 4,4814.6 hectares in the year 1988-89.

Atmakur, Koilakuntla and Dhone are some of the places where sericulture has some progress in the district.

The district has one high capacity grainage, three silk reeling units, five seed farms, six silkworm rearing units, one twisting unit and one cocoon market. Sericulture industry which was not known a decade ago, now it has become the livelihood for many farmers in this district.[24]

## Anantapur District

Anantapur district ranks first among mulberry raw silk producing districts in Andhra Pradesh. In spite of severe drought and low rainfall, mulberry cultivation in Anantapur has increased enormously. The success of sericulture in this backward district was largely attributed to DPAP introduced in the year 1975-76. A detailed study is represented in the following chapter.

## Conclusion

Thus, sericulture achieved prestigious place in Indian economy due to its advantages, associated with the well-being of small and marginal farmers. India is producing all the four known varities of silk and occupies a unique position among the silk producing nations in the world. In recent times, sericulture in India has undergone a tremendous change and has started wearing a new look. Till the begining of decade seventies, it used to be regarded as a subsidary or minor crop which provided additional income to the farmers. Now it has attained the status of an important cash crop along with sugarcane, cotton, tobacco. It is highly remunerative both under irrigated and rainfed conditions. The area under mulberry cultivation has been increasing every year. Karnataka and Andhra Pradesh States have emerged as major silk producing States in the country.

In Andhra Pradesh, the sericulture industry has spread its net to cover all the districts. The rapid expansion in the area under mulberry cultivation has taken place due to the sincere efforts of State Government in initiating and implementing speical development programmes for sericulture. In Andhra Pradesh, Mulberry cultivation is mainly concentrated in four district of Rayalaseema. Anantapur district is leading in the production of mulberry raw silk mainly due to implementation of DPAP and IRDP by the Government.

*Notes :*

1. C.S.B. Silk Companion, 1992, Bangalore, p.1.
2. D.V. Ramana, "Economics of Sericulture and Silk Industry in India", p. 27.
3. Muniraju, "Sericulture a tool for rural development", Souvenir on International Congress on Tropical Sericulture practices, February, 1988, Swiss Development Co-operation, New Delhi and Central Silk Board, India, pp.35.
4. D.V. Ramana, "Economics of Sericulture and Silk Industry in India", p.10
5. Ibid., p.16
6. C.S.B. Silkman's Companion, 1989, Bangalore, p. 42.
7. Indian Silk, February, 1992, p.5.
8. Indian Silk, January, 1991, p.6.
9. D.L. Narayana, "Economics of Sericulture in Rayalaseema", S.V. University, Tirupathi, 1979, p.81.
10. Indian Silk, October, 1991, p.35.
11. C.S.B. Silkman's Companion, Bangalore, p.9.
12. C.S.B. Silkman's companion, Bangalore, 1992.
13. J.F. Paharkar, "Sericulture in Andhra Pradesh all set for a big leap", Indian Silk, Vol. XXVIII, No. 5.
14. Asha Murthy, Sericulture in Andhra Pradesh, Souvenir on International Congress on Tropical Sericulture Practices, February, 1988, op. cit., p.8.
15. C.S.B. Silkman's Companion, 1989, op.cit., p.24.
16. Deputy Director, Department of Sericulture, Anantapur.
17. Md. Muneer Pasha, "Swiss aid to the mulberry sericulture development project in Andhra Pradesh and Tamil Nadu", Indian Silk, Vol. XXVII. No. 3, July, 1988, p. 26.

18. Smt. Asha Murthy, "Sericulture in Andhra Pradesh", Souvenir on International Congress on Tropical Sericulture Practices, February, 1988, op. cit., p. 95.
19. Joint Director, Department of Sericulture, Anantapur.
20. Ibid.
21. Ibid.
22. Ibid.
23. Joint Director, Department of Sericulture, Anantapur.
24. Joint Director, Department of Sericulture, Anantapur.

# Origin, Growth and Development of Sericulture

Sericulture activity provides scope to improve incomes of small and marginal farmers belonging to weaker sections and also provides gainful employment to the unemployed youth in the district. The soil and climate conditions of the district are also suitable to raise the mulberry crop which requires relatively minimum water facilities. Development of sericulture industry in Anantapur district took place only after 1974-75 i.e., by implementation of six-point formula and DPAP schemes. Out of 1,83,600 acres of total Andhra Pradesh mulberry acreage, Anantapur district alone is covering 74,500 acres by the end of August, 1991.[1] The total families engaged in this mulberry cultivation in Anantapur district is 50,648. In this chapter an attempt is made to analyse the development of sericulture in Anatapur district.

## Geographical Features

Anantapur district is situated in Rayalaseema region of Andhra Pradesh. It was formed in the year 1882 separating from Bellary district. This district lies between 13° 40' and 15° 15' north latitude and 76° 51' and 78° 30' east longitude. This is the southern most district of the Rayalaseema region. Anatapur district is surrounded on the east and the north by Cudapah and Kurnool district, respectively and Chittoor and Karnataka State are situated at its southern and western borders, respectively.[2]

Anantapur district has a fairly good elevation, which provides the district with tolerable climate throughout the year. The normal rainfall in the district is 520 mm. the least, when compared to Rayalaseema and other parts of Andhra Pradesh. The normal rainfall for the south-west monsoon period is 310.8 mm. which forms about 60 per cent of the total rainfall for the year. The failure of the rains in this critical south-west monsoon period of June to September will lead the district into frequent droughts. The rainfall for north-east monsoon period is 147.0 mm. only, which forms 28 per cent of the total rainfall for the year. The other months are almost dry. March, April and May are warm months where the daily maximum temperature ranges between 29.1$^0$C to 38.4$^0$C.[3]

The soil in Anantapur district are predominantly red (being the 76.5 per cent of the total area). Both under red and black soils clay and sandy nature exists.[4] Total geographical area of the district is 19.13 lakh hectares. Out of all districts in Andhra Pradesh, Anantapur occupies the second lowest position in respect of irrigation facilities. As per the survey conducted in 1984, ground water is available in an extent of 1,37,780 hectares metres in Anantapur district and only 24 per cent of the potential is under utility at present.[5]

The total population in the district in 1991 was 31.84 lakhs. The rural population was 76.49 per cent. The working force in the total population of the district forms 46.70 per cent out of the which 30 per cent are in the agriculture sector.[6]

## Development of Sericulture

Mulberry cultivation was first started at Veebhuthipalli village in Anantapur district. Now this village comes under Lapakshi mandal. The mulberry cultivation was started with

2 hectares. But the mulberry cultivation did not get any sort of improvement for a long time nearly two-and-half decades due to lack of proper knowledge and government assistance regarding sericulture. After implementation of DPAP, mulberry cultivation gained tremendous progress.

Prior to the implementation of DPAP in Anantapur district, a silk farm was established at Lepakshi in pursuance of the scheme "development of silk industry in Circar and Rayalaseema". Later the silk farm was shifted to Hidurpur in 1946, its work during the early years was in an experimental stage designed to find out whether mulberry cultivation and silkworm rearing could be successfully raised in this area. As the hectarage under mulberry cultivation was encouraging, a grainage was established at Hindupur in 1956-57 for preparation and supply of cross bread disease-free laying to the sericulturists.

During 1974-75, six-point formula programme came into operation for development of sericulture in Anantapur district. Under this programme an amount of Rs. 15.35 laks was allocated, out of which Rs. 14.68 lakhs was utilised for construction of foreign race seed farm at Penukonda and local race seed farm at Kadiri and for the creation of infrastructure facilities.[7]

The World Bank mission had conducted a survey in different districts and recommended Anantapur district to include among the six drought affected districts of India. The DPAP came into being in 1975. Sericulture is taken up as one of the important schemes. Sericulture has been identified as an effective tool for rural development.

There were hardly 3,560 mulberry growers in the district at that time. The industry had to pass through teething problems in regard to supply of mulberry cuttings and disease-free layings to farmers. The price of cocoons was low and could not attract the farmers initially. Marketing facilities were also poor. Despite vast potential, the major constraint was the meagre budget that restricted the vertical growth of the industry.

A gradual rise in the price of cocoons and incentives provided to the farmers for plantation, construction of rearing sheds, sinking of new wells and improvement in the supply in highly productive cross breeds, establishment of cocoon markets and adequate budget under DPAP provided ideal conditions for the progress of sericulture and now it has become a money spinner for small farmers in the district.

Mulberry is grown on small-scale basis. The total families engaged in this mulberry cultivation in Anantapur district is 50,400 by the end of August 1991. Anantapur is cocoon leading producer in the country, and maintains its present position. Already Anantapur has risen to the States first position and elevating the Andhra Pradesh to the second largest cocoon producer in the country.

It is evident from the Table 3.1. (Figure 3.1.) that during the year 1976-77, the financial allocation for the sericulture under DPAP in Anantapur district was Rs. 5.20 lakhs and it rose to Rs. 57.28 lakhs in 1988-89. During 1989-90 there was no allocation for the sericulture development under DPAP.

## Mulberry Cultivation

The entire area of mulberry cultivation in the district is under irrigated conditions. Irrigation is provided through borewells, open wells, and tanks. Hence, there is no mulberry cultivation under rainfed conditions in the district. Out of 31,235 hectares of mulberry, 14,453 hectares is planted with local variety and 16,782 hectares with high yielding variety of K2 or M5 mulberry cuttings. Steps are taken to replace local variety with M5 cuttings with wider spacing to increase leaf yields per hectare. Subsidy was also given to the small and marginal farmers to procure M5 cuttings. As already mentioned, mulberry is cultivation in 63 mandals of Anantapur district. The spread of mulberry, which depends on its intensity, is shown in the Table 3.2.

**Table 3.1 : Particulars of Financing to Sericulture Under Drought-Prone Programme in Anantapur District**

*(Rs. in Lakhs)*

| *Year* | *Allocation* | *Expenditure* | *Percentage of expenditure to allocation* |
|---|---|---|---|
| 1976–77 | 5.20 | 5.20 | 00.00 |
| 1977–78 | 41.74 | 11.00 | 26.35 |
| 1978–79 | 40.38 | 36.00 | 89.15 |
| 1979–80 | 78.81 | 56.04 | 71.11 |
| 1980–81 | 98.21 | 90.01 | 91.65 |
| 1981–82 | 60.07 | 35.80 | 59.60 |
| 1982–83 | 44.82 | 33.88 | 75.59 |
| 1983–84 | 65.55 | 64.99 | 99.15 |
| 1984–85 | 58.97 | 52.50 | 89.03 |
| 1985–86 | 31.10 | 30.75 | 98.87 |
| 1986–87 | 35.36 | 28.84 | 81.10 |
| 1987–88 | 22.95 | 21.75 | 94.77 |
| 1988–89 | 57.28 | 57.28 | 100.00 |
| 1989–90 | — | — | — |
| 1990–91 | 4.00 | 4.00 | 100.00 |
| 1991–92 | 2.90 | 2.25 | 77.59 |
| | | **Mean Percentage :** | **83.60** |

Source : Office of the Deputy Director, Department of Sericulture, Anantapur.

It is evident from Table 3.2 that there is huge increase in the area under mulberry cultivation from 1976-77 to 1991-92.

During the financial year 1991-92, 1,306 hectares of mulberry was planted. This raised the area planted with mulberry from 1,214 hectares in 1975-76 to 31,235 hectares by 1991-92, since inception of drought prone area programme. The district was categorised into six divisions for the conve-

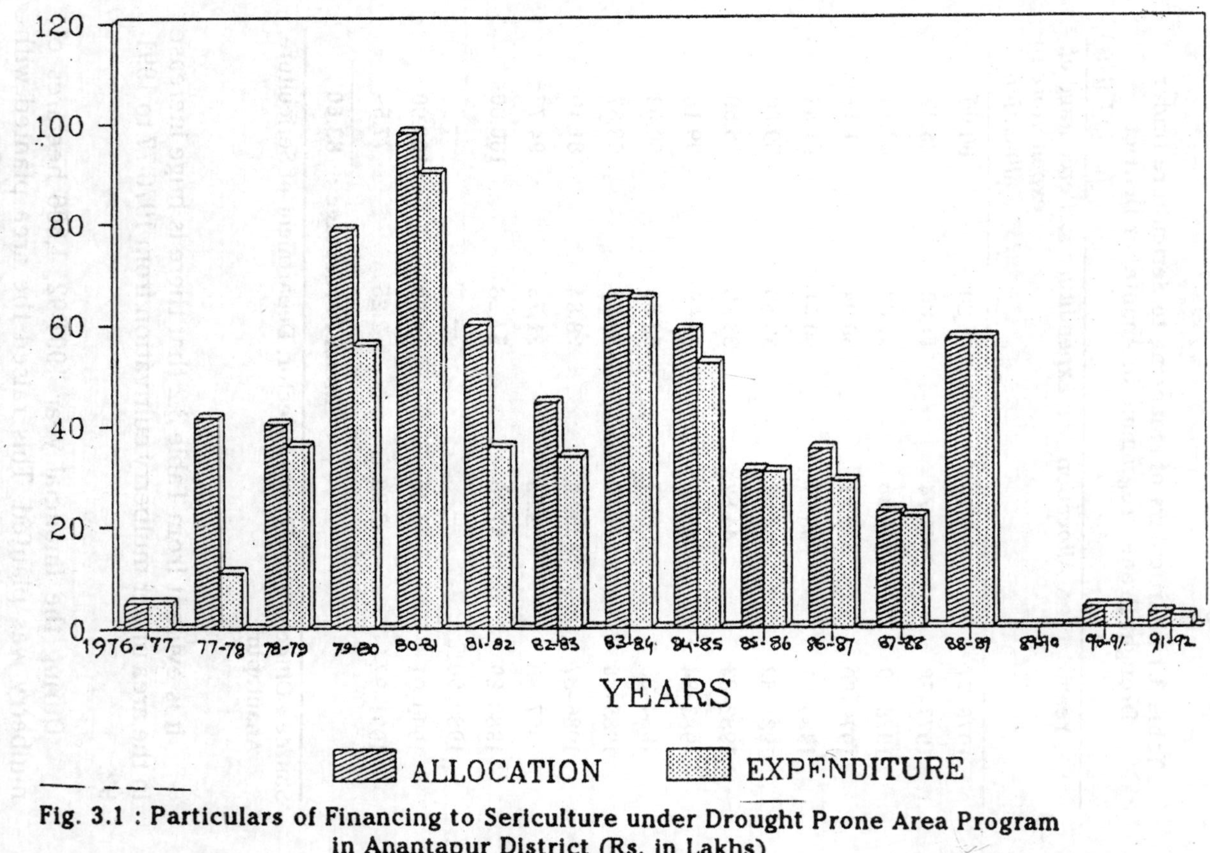


**Fig. 3.1 : Particulars of Financing to Sericulture under Drought Prone Area Program in Anantapur District (Rs. in Lakhs)**

**Table 3.2 : Area Brought Under Mulberry Cultivation in Anantapur District**

*(in Hectares)*

| Year | Achievement during the year | Achievement cumulative |
|---|---|---|
| 1976–77 | 592 | 1,086 |
| 1977–78 | 1,432 | 3,238 |
| 1978–79 | 2,521 | 5,759 |
| 1979–80 | 2,780 | 8,539 |
| 1980–81 | 3,243 | 11,782 |
| 1981–82 | 3,777 | 15,559 |
| 1982–83 | 3,857 | 19,416 |
| 1983–84 | 1,352 | 20,768 |
| 1984–85 | 895 | 21,663 |
| 1985–86 | 847 | 22,510 |
| 1986–87 | 1,222 | 23,732 |
| 1987–88 | 1,579 | 25,311 |
| 1988–89 | 1,641 | 26,952 |
| 1989–90 | 1,705 | 28,657 |
| 1990–91 | 1,272 | 29,929 |
| 1991–92 | 1,306 | 31,235 |

*Source* : Office of the Deputy Director, Department of Sericulture, Anantapur.

nience. The Table 3.3. (Figure 3.2) gives the division-wise distribution of area under mulberry cultivation in the district.

It is evident from the above table that the area under mulberry cultivation is high in Hindupur, Madakasira and Kadiri divisions, whereas Dharmavaram, Penukonda, Anantapur divisions show a gradual increase in sericulture adoption. The premier silk producing State in the country, Karnataka adjacent to the borders of Hindupur, Madakasira and kadiri has been a great boon for the rapid progress of sericulture in the above divisions. The progress of sericulture in the

**Table 3.3 : Division-wise Distribution of Area Under Mulberry Cultivation 1991–92**

| *Sl. No.* | *Name of the Division* | *Area under Mulberry Cultivation (in hectares)* |
|---|---|---|
| 1. | Dharmavaram (Dharmavaram, C.K. Palli, Kothacheruvu) | 4,721 |
| 2. | Hindupur (Hindupur) | 7,913 |
| 3. | Kadiri (Kadiri East and Kadiri West) | 5,961 |
| 4. | Madakasira (Madakasira) | 7,540 |
| 5. | Anantapur (Kudair, Singanamala, Gooty Uravakonda, Tadpatri) | 2,410 |
| 6. | Penukonda | 2,690 |
| | **Total** | **31,235** |

Source : Office of the Deputy Direcor, Department of Sericulture, Anantpaur.

above division is spreading to all the villages in Anantapur district.

## Infrastructure

The infrastructure has helped a lot for the progress of sericulture in the district. The complete details of infrastructure before and after the implementation of drought prone area programme are furnished in the Table 3.4.

After the implementation of DPAP in the district, there was a steep rise in the infrastructure facilities provided for sericulture. Before DPAP, there were two grainage centres with 10 lakh capacity, one seed farm and one chawkie rearing unit. After DPAP, now three high capacity grainage centres at Hindupur, Kadiri, Madakasira, three cocoon markets, eight chawkie rearing units, six silk reeling units one semi-automatic reeling, twelve farmers silkworm hatchery centres, three twisting units, one regional training centre, ten cross breed disease free laying centres are also established. So as to

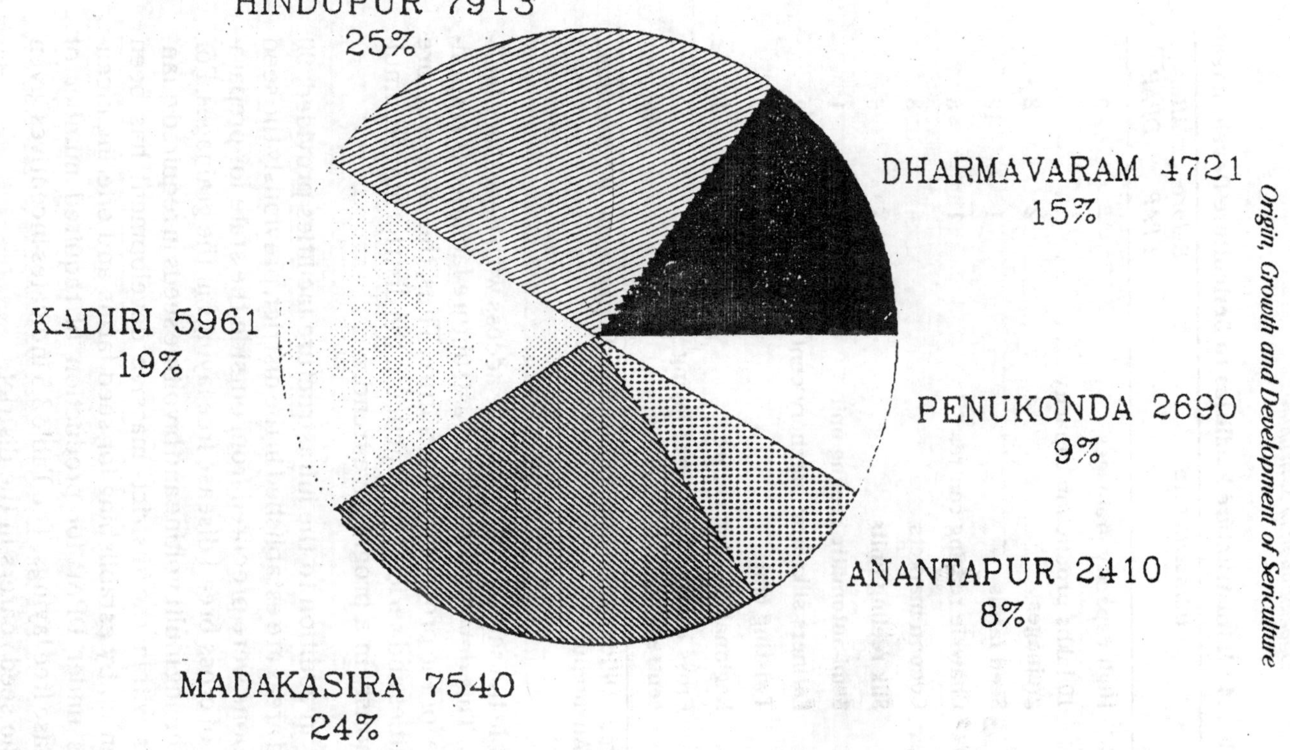


**Fig. 3.2 : Division-wise Distribution of Area Under Mulberry Cultivation during 1991–92 (in Hectares)**

**Table 3.4 : Infrastructure Facilities to Sericulture Development**

| *Sl. No.* | *Infrastructure* | *Before DPAP* | *After DPAP* |
|---|---|---|---|
| 1. | High capacity grainages | – | 3 |
| 2. | 10 lakhs production capacity grainages | 2 | 8 |
| 3. | Seed farms | 1 | 12 |
| 4. | Chawkie rearing centres | 1 | 8 |
| 5. | Cocoon markets | – | 3 |
| 6. | Silk reeling units | – | 6 |
| 7. | Semi-automatic reeling unit | – | 1 |
| 8. | Farmers silkworm hatchery centre | – | 12 |
| 9. | Twisting units | – | 3 |
| 10. | Regional training centre | – | 1 |
| 11. | Cross breed disease free laying centres | – | 10 |

*Source* : Office of the Deputy Director, Department of Sericulture, Anantapur.

enable the sericulturists to have access with necessary facilities. This development in infrastructure facilities is responsible for the progress of sericulture. Thus, the infrastructure facilities and sericulture practice in the district moved simultaneously in a progressive trend.

In addition to the infrastructure facilities provided, 90 seed areas are established in the district, previously the seed cocoons were procured from outside the state for preparation of cross bread disease free layings in the grainages. For producing multi-voltine and bivoltine seeds in required quantities within the district, massive development has been taken up by establishing for seed farms and offering incentives under DPAP for production of required number of disease free layings. The Table 3.5 indicates incentives given to the seed rearers in the district.

**Table 3.5 : Incentives to the Seed Rearers**

*(Rs. in lakhs)*

| *Sl. No.* | *Details* | *Amount sanctioned* |
|---|---|---|
| 1. | 50 per cent subsidy for construction of rearing sheds to 761 seed rearers, Rs. 2,500 each | 19.03 |
| 2. | 50 per cent subsidy for purpose of rearing equipment to 561 seed rearers, Rs.1,500 each | 8.42 |
| 3. | 50 per cent subsidy for purchase of chemical fertilizers to 750 seed rearers, Rs. 520 each. | 3.75 |
| 4. | Crop insurance to seed rearers on payment of 50 per cent premium. | 4.31 |
| 5. | Supply of nylon nets on 100 per cent subsidy to 175 seed rears in the district | 0.35 |
| 6. | Bonus to L,R, seed rearers for excess production of L, R, seed cocoons, Rs.10 per kg. for 10,000 kgs. | 1.00 |
| 7. | Bonus to bivoltine seed rearers Rs. 5 per kg. | 1.63 |
| | **Total** | **38.49** |

Source : Office of the Deputy Director, Department of Sericulture, Anantpaur.

In addition to all the above incentives, assistance for inwell-bores on 100 per cent subsidy and subsidy is also provided to 112 open wells in both multi-voltine and bivoltine seed areas under drought relief programme.

## Seed Cocoon Pproduction

After implementation of DPAP the development of seed areas, with all necessary incentives, the district has become self-sufficient in the production of both multivoltine and bivoltine cocoons. The seed cocoon production in the seed areas was increasing year after year. These facts are furnished in Table 3.6.

It is evident from Table 3.6, that the production of seed cocoons is higher in seed areas than in the farms. Both multi-

**Table 3.6 : Seed Cocoon Production 1983–1992**

| Year | Seed Cocoons Production in the seed area | | Seed Cocoon Production in the farms | |
|---|---|---|---|---|
| | Multivoltine | Bivoltine | Multivoltine | Bivoltine |
| 1982–83 | 1,29,56,750 | 38,25,700 | 4,93,400 | 41,050 |
| 1983–84 | 1,38,37,860 | 43,12,600 | 3,97,940 | 1,09,318 |
| 1984–85 | 1,47,16,623 | 39,06,852 | 5,93,440 | 3,68,860 |
| 1985–86 | 2,06,17,960 | 92,54,618 | 6,65,305 | 5,12,240 |
| 1986–87 | 3,14,63,000 | 73,79,000 | 12,84,332 | 4,00,280 |
| 1987–88 | 4,52,38,000 | 11,74,300 | 8,28,870 | 6,77,842 |
| 1988–89 | 5,90,29,000 | 2,50,68,000 | 16,10,000 | 9,71,055 |
| 1990–91 | 6,52,69,000 | 3,95,00,000 | 14,12,584 | 8,95,876 |
| 1991–92 | 11,75,31,000 | 4,64,36,000 | 17,08,851 | 9,70,651 |

*Source* : Office of the Deputy Director, Department of Sericulture, Anantapur.

voltine and bivoltine seed cocoons are produced. But, multivoltine seed cocoons production was two times higher than the bivoltine seed cocoon production. Up to 2989-90 there was an increasing trend in the production of multivoltine seed cocoons. During the year 1989-91, there was a declining trend in the production of multivoltine seed cocoons. Again from 1990-91, the production of multivoltine was increased.

In bivoltine seed cocoon production, number of fluctuations were occurred up to 1987-88. From 1988-89 onwards there was no backward shift in the production of bivoltine seed cocoons.

To provide marketing facilities to the seed cocoons produced by the seed rearers, one multivoltine seed cocoon market was established at Gorantla during 1986-87. The multivoltine cocoons produced by the seed rearers will come to the said market and the person in-charge of grainage. They procure their required quantities for preparation of cross bread disease free layings. The seed cocoons rate will be fixed by the inspector of sericulture, based on the norms communicated by the Andhra Pradesh Seed Committee.

## Silkworm Egg Production

There were only two grainages in Anantapur district before the implementation of DPAP, one at Hindupur and another at Kadiri, with a production capacity of 5 lakhs each. The requirement of cross breed disease free layings was 10.92 lakhs per annum. As the hectarage under mulberry in the district is increasing year after year, the demand for cross breed disease free layings has also increased simultaneously to 6 crores to meet this increased demand. Three high capacity grainage centres at Hindupur, Kadiri and Madakasira and eight small capacity grainage centres were established at different places.

The three high capacity grainages were provided with cold storage facilities. The cost of each storage plant comes to Rs. 6.50 lakhs which was also included in the financial implications shown in the Table 3.7.

**Table 3.7 : Particulars of Financial Implications and Production Capacities of the Grainages in Anantapur District**

| *Sl. No.* | *Name of the grainage* | *Allocation (Rs. in lakhs)* | *Production capacity (No. in lakhs)* |
|---|---|---|---|
| 1. | Three high capacity grainages at Hindupur, Kadiri and Madakasira | 88.50 | 90.00 |
| 2. | Eight small capacity grainages at Hindurpur, Kadiri, Madakasira, Penukonda, Dharmavaram, Anantapur, Kalyandurg and Rayadurg | 21.60 | 80.00 |
| | **Total** | **110.10** | **170.00** |

*Source* : Office of the Deputy Director, Department of Sericulture, Anantapur.

The year-wise Cross Breed Disease Free Layings (CBDFLs) production in the district since inception of DPAP is shown in the Table 3.8.

**Table 3.8 : Production Particulars of CBDFLs in Anantapur District**

| *Year* | *Production (in lakh kgs.)* |
|---|---|
| 1976–77 | 11.70 |
| 1977–78 | 24.06 |
| 1978–79 | 30.14 |
| 1979–80 | 56.81 |
| 1980–81 | 72.17 |
| 1981–82 | 56.92 |
| 1982–83 | 53.69 |
| 1983–84 | 41.11 |
| 1984–85 | 60.07 |
| 1985–86 | 69.77 |
| 1986–87 | 73.16 |
| 1987–88 | 95.02 |
| 1988–89 | 105.12 |
| 1989–90 | 109.12 |
| 1990–91 | 107.94 |
| 1991–92 | 165.40 |

Source : Office of the Deputy Director, Department of Sericulture, Anantapur.

It is evident from the Table 3.8 that the production of CBDFLs in the district has increased steeply up to 1980-81 and in the subsequent years, production fluctuates due to severe drought conditions prevailed in the district and again from 1986-87 onwards the production started increasing gradually.

## Reeling Cocoon Production

The yield of reeling cocoons per 100 disease free layings will be 40 to 45 kg. On an average, 2,000 to 3,000 laying can be brushed per hectare per annum. So it is calculated that 800 to 1,200 kg. of cocoon yield can be obtained from one hectare per annum. The cocoon production after the implementation of DPAP has gone up in the district. The trends in reeling cocoon production are shown in the Table 3.9.

**Table 3.9 : Reeling Cocoon Production in Anantapur District**

| *Year* | *Cocoon Production (in lakh kgs.)* |
|---|---|
| 1976–77 | 4.00 |
| 1977–78 | 14.00 |
| 1978–79 | 25.30 |
| 1979–80 | 50.82 |
| 1980–81 | 77.21 |
| 1981–82 | 85.12 |
| 1982–83 | 92.11 |
| 1983–84 | 101.09 |
| 1984–85 | 70.60 |
| 1985–86 | 72.81 |
| 1986–87 | 79.50 |
| 1987–88 | 111.32 |
| 1988–89 | 124.00 |
| 1989–90 | 135.61 |
| 1990–91 | 147.37 |
| 1991–92 | 117.13 |

Source : Office of the Deputy Director, Department of Sericulture, Anantapur.

The particulars furnished in the table reveal that the cocoon production has increased year after year up to 1983-84 and during 1984-85 the production of reeling cocoons fell due to severe drought. Again from 1985-86 onwards the production of reeling cocoons has been increasing gradually.

The silk yarn produced by bivoltine cocoons is of high quality than the yarn produced by multivoltine cocoons. The bivoltine silk yarn is having more demand in the international silk market. One semi-automatic reeling unit was established to Anantapur under DPAP for the production of bivoltine silk. In addition to that a few more units have come up in private sector. To meet the regular demand of the reeling unit, production of bivoltine cocoons is very essential. Bivoltine programmes have been taken up in the district in an area of 486 hectares. The quantity of bivoltine cocoon produced in the district has been increasing.

## Marketing

Previously the sericulturists in the district used to transport and market their cocoons to Karnataka cocoon markets. From 1978-79 onwards some of the local people have started private cocoon markets and used to collect two per cent commission from both the reelers and rearers. So the government has established cocoon markets at Hindupur, Kadiri and Dharmavaram under the provision of Andhra Pradesh Silkworm Seed Cocoon Control Act, 1956 to avoid the influence of middle men in cocoon transactions and provide fair market facility to the cocoons produced. An amount of Rs. 10.50 lakhs was incurred for the establishment of each cocoon market. The cocoon market started functioning from April 1983. So far 93,163 tonnes of reeling cocoons valued at Rs. 14,43,503 were transacted and an amount of Rs. 288.91 lakhs was derived as market fee by the government.

The year-wise value of cocoons transacted and market fee collected since inception are furnished.

The Table 3.10 makes it clear that the cocoon markets are getting huge revenue to the State Government and existing more service to the public. Up to 1991-92, 231.63 lakh kg. cocoons were transacted. Market fee collected during this transaction was Rs. 288.91 lakhs. In 1983-84, 29.68 lakh kg. of cocoons were transacted and the quantity of cocoons transacted has been fluctuating in the subsequent years. This happened because of imperfections and lack of knowledge about the prices prevailing as the markets which are situated in distance places.

## Financial Assistance

Loan scheme was introduced under DPAP to encourage the farmers to take up mulberry cultivation and to provide financial assistance to the new sericulturists. Under this scheme loans are provided to the small and marginal farmers for mulberry plantation, purchase of rearing equipment and for the construction of rearing sheds. Under this scheme

**Table 3.10 : Marketing of Cocoons**

| *Year* | *Quality of Cocoons transacted (in lakh kgs.)* | *Value of cocoons transacted (Rs. in lakhs)* | *Market fee collected (Rs. in lakhs)* |
|---|---|---|---|
| 1983–84 | 29.68 | 1,056.16 | 21.36 |
| 1984–85 | 20.97 | 803.38 | 16.70 |
| 1985–86 | 19.31 | 868.84 | 17.39 |
| 1986–87 | 22.40 | 937.85 | 18.77 |
| 1987–88 | 20.08 | 1,076.27 | 21.55 |
| 1988–89 | 21.32 | 1,380.15 | 27.60 |
| 1989–90 | 30.50 | 2,176.13 | 43.02 |
| 1990–91 | 35.06 | 2,449.67 | 48.78 |
| 1991–92 | 32.31 | 3,686.58 | 73.74 |
| **Total** | **231.63** | **14,435.03** | **288.91** |

Source : Office of the Deputy Director, Department of Sericulture, Anantapur.

subsidy was also provided by the government to the extent of 25 per cent to small farmers and $33^1/_3$ per unit to the marginal farmers and loan portion was given by the financial institutions. Institutional finance was made available by Co-operative Agricultural Development Bank, commercial bank and other agencies. Commercial banks had begun taking interest in sericulture and started financing since 1975-76. Their schemes provide financial assistance to sericulturists for construction of rearing houses, digging wells and acquiring related equipment, maintenance of mulberry gardens, rearing of silkworms and the reeling of silk etc., thereby covering long tem, medium term as well as short term needs of the sericulturists.

It is also evident from the Table 3.11 that from 1983-84 onwards loans have been sanctioned under IRDP and DPAP. The number of beneficiaries in 1978-79 were only 450 and it went up to 1,078 members in 1991-92, showing an increase of

**Table 3.11 : Financial Assistance to Sericulturists**

*(Rs. in lakhs)*

| *Sl. No.* | *Year* | *Number of* cultivators benefited | *Loan* portion | *Amount of* subsidy released |
|---|---|---|---|---|
| 1. | 1978–79 | 450 | 18.00 | 6.00 |
| 2. | 1979–80 | 674 | 19.13 | 6.37 |
| | <u>IRDP</u> | | | |
| 1. | 1983–84 | 899 | 37.79 | 13.58 |
| 2. | 1984–85 | 342 | 23.60 | 7.87 |
| 3. | 1985–86 | 381 | 26.50 | 8.88 |
| 4. | 1986–87 | 265 | 24.50 | 8.20 |
| 5. | 1987–88 | 693 | 65.80 | 22.29 |
| 6. | 1988–89 | 983 | 66.38 | 25.19 |
| 7. | 1989–90 | 2,003 | 193.20 | 74.802 |
| 8. | 1990–91 | 1,500 | 130.226 | 56.096 |
| 9. | 1991–92 | 1,078 | 93.165 | 40.918 |

Source : Office of the Deputy Director, Department of Sericulture, Anantapur.

more than cent per cent. Accordingly, the loan portion sanctioned also increased from Rs. 18.00 lakhs (1978-79) to Rs. 93.16 lakhs (1991-92). The amount of subsidy was only Rs. 6 lakh in 1978-79. It has increased to Rs. 40.91 lakhs. All these above figures indicate the growing tendency towards sericulture in the district.

To derive maximum financial assistance, 150 Cooperative Societies were formed during the month of September 1989 in Anantapur district. Each society consists of 100 members having not more than two hectares of mulberry cultivation. These societies work under the organisation of "Rashtra Karshak Parishad". The Executive Committee of each society consists of eight members, seven directors and one Chief Promoter. These societies undertake various projects for the benefit of sericulturists.

## Employment

Sericulture industry is providing direct livelihood for over 3.30 lakh people in the district. The demand for hired labour is increasing every year. Family labour involvement in sericulture activities is decreasing as there is an improvement in the living standards of the sericulturists. The Table 3.12 reveals the entire picture of the number of persons involved in sericulture in the district.

**Table 3.12 : Employment Generation in Sericulture in Anantapur District 1991–92**

| *Sl. No.* | *Name of the division* | *Scheduled Caste* | *Scheduled Tribe* | *Backward Caste* | *Other Caste* | *Total* |
|---|---|---|---|---|---|---|
| 1. | Hindupur | 918 | 610 | 8,170 | 7,206 | 16,904 |
| 2. | Madakasira | 811 | 244 | 2,537 | 7,856 | 11,448 |
| 3. | Kadiri | 494 | 486 | 2,693 | 5,636 | 9,309 |
| 4. | Dharmavaram | 328 | 258 | 2,390 | 3,705 | 6,681 |
| 5. | Penukonda | 298 | 139 | 1,481 | 2,277 | 4,195 |
| 6. | Anantapur | 566 | 30 | 569 | 946 | 2,111 |
| | **Total** | **3,415** | **1,767** | **17,840** | **27,626** | **50,648** |

*Source* : Office of the Deputy Director, Department of Sericulture, Anantapur.

It is evident from the Table 3.12 that the number of persons engaged in sericulture were high in Hindupur with 33.37 per cent of the total sericulture families of the district. Madakasira division stands second with 22.60 per cent. Kadiri, Dharmavaram, Penukonda and Anantapur divisions occupy third, fourth, fifth and last places respectively. The Scheduled Castes and the Scheduled Tribes families under sericulture are only 3,415 and 1,767 respectively. Out of the total 50,648 sericulture families, forward caste people are dominating with 54.54 per cent, while backward classes occupy second place with 35.22 per cent and the rest are Scheduled Castes and Scheduled Tribes. So it can be concluded that sericulture is being practised by all people in the district though it is predominantly in the hands of upper castes and backward classes.

## Conclusion

With the implementation of DPAP, sericulture in Anantapur district has made tremendous progress though drought has been a recurring feature of the district. The climatic conditions are conducive for silkworm rearing and cocoon breeding. The suitability of sericulture in the district has initiated many of the small and marginal farmers to shift from other traditional crops to sericulture.

The area under mulberry has increased from 1,214 hectares in 1975-76 to 31,235 hectares in 1991-92. Towards sericulture development in the district, DPAP has enhanced financial allocation from an amount of Rs. 5.20 lakhs in 1976-77 to Rs. 57.28 lakhs in 1988-89. After 1988-89, there was backward shift in the financial allocation under DPAP. Infrastructure facilities were also provided under DPAP and as many as ten seed farms and three high capacity grainages were established. With the optimum utilisation of the available infrastructure, the raw silk production in Anantapur district during 1991-92 was as high as 11,49,641 kg. under both government and private sector which accounts for 33 per cent of total raw silk produced in the State. However, the credit for rapid progress of sericulture in the district goes to the efforts made by the government through DPAP by increasing the flow of funds under different schemes.

*Notes :*

1. Brief note on sericulture development in Anantapur district for the bankers workshop, pp.1.
2. Chief Planning Officer, *Hand Book of Statistics, 1987-88*, Anantapur district, District Statical Office, Anantapur, p.1.
3. *Ibid.*, p.3.
4. Office of the Deputy Director, Department of Sericulture,

5. *Ibid.*, p.6.
6. Chief Planning Officer, Anantapur.
7. Office of the Deputy Director, Development of Sericulture, Anantapur.

# Causative Factors For the Development of Sericulture

Sericulture is being practised in the entire district of Anantapur, but it is mainly concentrated in Hindupur, Kadiri, Madakasira, Penukonda, Dharmavaram and Anantapur divisions. Anantapur district has suitable loomed soils for mulberry cultivation. Moreover, majority of the farmers are vexed with traditional crops because of their frequent failures due to drought. Though sericulture needs more investment in the initial stage for its establishment and maintenance, yield would be sufficient for sustenance eve in severe drought conditions. It not only gives more income but employment. In view of the potentialities the area under mulberry is about to increase in the near future. The demand for silk is also increasing every year both in India and abroad. Anantapur has already reached first place in the State in producing mulberry raw silk. Under these favorable conditions, there is a better scope for the development of sericulture in Anantapur district.

To meet the raising demand for silk ( both in domestic and abroad) the Government of India is implementing a five-year project to develop sericulture with the financial assistance from World Bank. In this context Anantapur district is given priority in the allotment of funds. Necessary amount will be provided for sanctioning loans, subsidies and incentives to the sericulturists.

In order to provide necessary infrastructure to the sericulturists, additional facilities such as seed farms, markets and reeling units are proposed to be created. This include establishment of one reeling industry and grainages under private sector, two twisting units and establishment of silk exchange in public sector and Research and Training Institute at Rachepalli of Hindupur mandal.

Regarding incentives, 10 per cent of unit cost irrespective of the size of the land holding is proposed to sanction under IRDP. Moreover, the sericulturists are provided with necessary monetary assistance for drilling of surface bore wells and deepening of open wells and for purchasing of pump sets of lift water from wells. The seed rearers also be given benefit with 50 per cent of subsidy on shed and equipment.

The growth of sericulture in Anantapur district would accelerate with the assistance from the World Bank Project and help in improving the standard of living of a number of small and marginal farmers in the district.

## Adaptable to Different Environments

In Andhra Pradesh, sericulture is practised mostly in the districts of Anantapur and Chittoor, that too in the elevated hilly regions. Of late, it has been noticed that mulberry is a hardy plant that can survive even in drought prone and warmer regions. As a result, the activity is gaining importance in these areas and also in the hot costal plains where temperature remains around 100$^{0}$F in summer. It has also been realised that the risk of crop failures is less in the case of sericulture. To reduce the incident of the high temperature on the silkworm some indigenous cooling systems like improvised running perforated hoses at the top of rearing sheds to facilitates dripping of water, installation of fans to blow cool air through wet gunnies and even air-coolers are adopted in the district.

## Quick Returns

To start with mulberry crop takes only six months to mature and thereafter four to six crops can be had in a year. The leaves can be sold to silkworm rearers if the grower himself cannot rear silkworm and sell the cocoons with better profits. Crops like sugarcane of jute take a year to give the yield and cotton about eight months. Paddy can be raised twice in a year. Even in the case of non-mulberry sericulture, the number of yields in a year are many, depending upon the type of silkworm and the food plant. Thus, sericulture is a source of recurring cash returns in the district, which enables the agriculturists to finance their operations without much resource to debt.

## Returns Per Acre

The Rayalaseema survey also reveals that per acre net return from sericulture is more than 2½ per cent times than that of sugarcane. Even in the case of double cropping of groundnut or paddy, gross returns will be less than that of the sericulture.

The returns are comparatively low from sugarcane, paddy and groundnut crops require on valuable inputs of water and land. Sericulture makes an economic use of these two valuable resources and ensures for higher returns than any of the present uses of water namely, paddy, sugarcane and groundnut. The net return per acre from sericulture is higher by five times over paddy, four times over sugarcane and two one-third times over groundnut, shown in Table 4.1

The above analysis shows that an acre of mulberry yields comparatively high return to the farmers and provides full time employment throughout the year. Sericulture thus, raises both the income and employment.

**Table 4.1 : Returns per Acre**

| *Sl. No.* | *Crop* | *Net return per acre* | *Water requirement of crops in inches* | *Net returns per acre inch of water (times)* |
|---|---|---|---|---|
| 1. | Paddy | 1,383 | 70 | 20 |
| 2. | Sugarcane | 2,168 | 80 | 27 |
| 3. | Groundnut | 657 | 15 | 44 |
| 4. | Sericulture | 6,770 | 65 | 104 |

Source : Economics of Sericulture in Rayalaseema, p. 90.

## Comparison with High Completion Crops

An analysis of comparative advantages of sericulture requires a comparison of the employment generation per acre, with the competing crops in the district. However, in analysing labour units required for a particular crop, due to consideration must be given the differences in the soil and agricultural practices. To be scientific, a special enquiry into labour inputs in fields of uniform soil fertility as well as agricultural efficiency, customs and practices under homogeneous conditions - is necessary to evaluate correctly the labour inputs for judging the employment potential of different crops. Scientific studies under homogeneous conditions may not be necessary what is needed is an exercise which would give broad indication of the quantity of employment generation under different crops in the district.

Data relating to labour input required, per acre in the cultivation of major crops of Anantapur district such as paddy, sugarcane and groundnut are taken. Cropping pattern in the district reveals the wide differences in labour input among the crops. The Table 4.2 shows representative data on employment potential of groundnut, paddy, sugarcane and sericulture crops (raised) in the district. Among all crops sericulture provides maximum employment and groundnut with least employment.

**Table 4.2 : Labour (Man-days) Requirement of Important Crops per Acre**

*(Unit : 1 acre)*

| *Sl. No.* | *Crop* | *Per crop employment* |
|---|---|---|
| 1. | Groundnut | 52 |
| 2. | Paddy | 98 |
| 3. | Sugarcane | 141 |
| 4. | Sericulture | 120* |

*Note* : * A minimum of four crops were raised in agricultural year.

*Source* : D.V. Ramana, Economics of Sericulture and Silk Industry in India, P. 35

The table shows that the input of labour, per acre of sericulture is more than three time that of sugarcane which is an annual crop. Even in the case of double cropping of paddy or groundnut, labour requirement are less than sericulture. Indeed, the labour requirements in mulberry gardening per acre, is nearly 2½ times that of paddy and 4½ times that of groundnut under double cropping. Further, in the cultivation of these crops the employment of labour is periodic and fluctuating, thereby resulting in seasonal unemployment. But sericulture provides employment throughout the year to the family labour, hence, sericulture provides stable and more employment opportunities to rural people.

In a country like ours, where 80 per cent of the population live in rural areas, largely dependent on agriculture, the vital role played by sericulture which is a agro-based employment oriented industry needs hardly emphasised. As a result of the improvement effected in recent years, the sericulture industry has established its economic superiority over other competing crops with a highly satisfactory cost benefit ratio. Pursuit of the sericulture in one hectare of irrigated land will provide full employment to ten persons (2 families—a family of 5 each) and provide them a net earning of around Rs. 8,000 to Rs. 9,000 per annum at the current costs of production and sale value of products. Besides, the sericulture industry is particularly suited to small and marginal farmers who grow their mulberry and undertake rearing of silk worms.

## Employment Effects

Further sericulture basically engages women and also the old and handicapped members of the cultivators families. In fact, while rearing, the entire family of the sericulture is involved. Hence, rearing generates less paid employment, though available farm servants are used for mulberry cultivation as for any other work and extra labour is hired for three or four days of picking at the period in the cycle of rearing when demand for leaves is at its maximum and household labour resources tend to become inadequate. As it is possible to raise five to six crops in a year, the family employment is distributed evenly over the years. In other words, sericulture activity has a most significant effect on the employment of family labour. Thus, farm labourer is able to find employment all year round by combing work in mulberry cultivation with silkworm rearing. To be precise, development of sericulture creates employment opportunities at the rate of not less than 1½ persons, per acre of mulberry cultivation and rearing, assuming 300 working days per farm labourer for a year.

It is very interesting to note that mulberry cultivation and silk worm rearing provide employment throughout the year to the farmer. Yet another noteworthy feature of sericulture activity is that nearly 50 per cent of the cultivators practising it are small and marginal farmers and the average size of the land holding, under mulberry is hardly 1.04 acre.[1] Sericulture is, thus, a most suitable and productive occupation for small and marginal farmers.

## Indirect Employment Effects

The whole area of raw silk industry, in the broadest sense, will also provide new employment. In silk reeling activity, there is a considerable scope for employment generation to the artisans and unskilled workers of rural areas.

A reeler, with a unit of 10 basins, provides employment, to 21 persons, including the reeler. The organisations of silk reeling and silk weaving can also help a many handloom weavers who have formed a vulnerable sections of the society in the rural areas with the introduction of cheap and attractive mill made cloth. Mulberry cultivation and associated activities will provide full employment not only to the small and marginal farmers but also to village artisans. The silk waste and pupae, the by-products of silk industry, open yet another sector of economic activities keeping people busy in processing and spinning of silk waste, producing pupae oil and pupae meal. The return from by-product adds to the profits of the primary producers besides giving jobs to many.

For the better yields from sericulture, the quality silkworm are the most essential. Silk spinning, weaving, dyeing and marketing etc., and by-product sector go on creating jobs. And there will be a further multiplier effect throughout the rest of the economy. If the job opportunities created in the construction of irrigation wells, rearing houses, rapid and replacement of rearing equipment, reeling, marketing, transport, extension research etc., with all their forward and backward linkage are considered, the employment potential of sericulture will be enormous. Finally, if the increased rural incomes from the sericulture industry are distributed fairly and evenly, they should increase the demand for kinds of consumer goods that can be produced domestically—furniture, utensils, bicycles etc. These goods have the additional advantages that they can be made in relatively labour activity at each stage of production process is evaluated taking into account all its ramifications and linkages - the result would surely be helpful in setting appropriate employment and output goods.

One of the factors responsible for concentration of sericulture is the favorable climatic condition conducive for silkworm rearing and breeding in Anantapur district.

The second reason is that the district is close to the State Karnataka where sericulture has made rapid strides, with frequent visits to neighboring places in Karnataka where sericulture is prospering. The people of Anantapur have acquired skills required to raise sericulture in the district.

Absence of scope for alternative crop enterprise is another factor for the farmers in the district to go in for sericulture. It is only since the completion of Tungabhadra irrigation project, crop diversification and intensive cultivation have been taking place in some mandals of Anantapur district. However, the benefits of canal irrigation are not found in the mandals where the sericulture is presently concentrated in the district.

Above all a more powerful factor accounting for the accelerated growth of sericulture was due to additional finances made available under five year plan programme for the improvement of drought prone district like Anantapur.

It is noted earlier that the acreage under mulberry cultivation was very much accelerated in the district since 1970.

# Problems of Sericulturists in India

Though sericulture in Anantapur district is showing rapid progress during the past 15 years, mulberry farmers are facing some problems pertaining to its organisation, marketing, finance, technology and extension.

The researcher has made an interview from the officials of sericulture department and sericulturists in the district. The following are the major problems.

## Availability of Layings

Generally sericulturists buy layings (CBDFLs) from the government grainages and licensed seed producers. The availability of these layings is adequate round the year except in summer season. The grainages already existing are inadequate in number and often fail to meet the demand. Hence, the sericulturists obtain layings, either from nearby Karnataka State Grainages or from private grainages. To meet the growing demand, grainages for local silkworm race have also to be set-up. Moreover, the government had to take interest to introduce bivoltine layings for commercial rearing in this district, as no such effort has been made so far.

## Shortage of Labour

Labour shortage is another problem expressed by the respondents. In spite of its employment potential, the sericulturists are suffering from shortage of labour. 10 per cent farmers expressed that it may because of the reason that mulberry cultivation can be done even in small segments of land holding. Hence, agriculture labour who won less than 0.20 hectares are also cultivating mulberry and silkworm rearing and thereby creating labour shortage for big farmers. The labour shortage in cultivating mulberry can be filled by introducing appropriate machinery in the mulberry fields on co-operative basis. The State Government should help farmers to overcome this problem.

## Finance for Investment

Financial assistance plays an important role in promoting mulberry cultivation and rearing of cocoons. The normal sericulturist is either a small farmer or a marginal farmer with limited means. There is need to secure adequate finance for making higher investment in sericulture. Sericulturists have to borrow from other sources like friends, relatives and private money lenders at higher rates of interest. Hence, for an orderly development of sericulture, the institutional agencies should identify the special features and needs of sericulturists and the extent of finance required for fixed and working capital.

## Problems of Disease and Pests of Mulberry and Silkworms

There are number of diseases which affect the normal growth of mulberry. The infected leaves are not suitable for silkworm rearing. Finding out the diseases in perfect time and utilisation of the preventive methods leads to so many difficulties for the poor farmers. Hence, the Government Departments should supply the preventive medicines at lesser rates to the farmers together with the sprayers. Recently Uzy fly is causing considerable damage to silkworms leading to heavy losses to the cocoon growers. The only method of control against this fly is to prevent the entry of the fly into the rearing room by providing wire mesh of suitable size for doors, windows and ventilators. This is to be intimated to all the cocoon growers in the district.

## Climatic Disturbances

Cool climatic throughout the year is a prerequisite for silkworm rearing, cocoon production and high renditta. Climatic disturbances upset the realisation of sericulture productivity. It is advised to adopt in the hot tropical climate especially during summer, new techniques like the use of air coolers, dripping of water on the rearing sheds, arranging the rearing rooms under the shade of big trees etc. The adoption of these techniques though increases the cost of production marginally, but reduces adverse effects on the quantity and quality of cocoons and income per hectare of mulberry farm. High leaf yield from mulberry garden located in good soil with irrigation facilities may compensate for the higher cost arising out of the extreme summer climate. In any case climatic hazards add to the drudgery of silkworm rearing necessitating greater care and attention to be shown by the sericulturists.

Hence, other things being equal, hot climate is a deterrent for sericulture entrepreneurship. As sericulture is a labour-intensive enterprise, high wages that prevail in the agricultural growth centres also constitute an obstacle for sericulture expansion. Big farmers, though they possess better capacity to face the climatic hazards, may not like the increased managerial responsibility and time required to look after the sericulture. Small farmers lack resources to provide adequate facilities to counteract the hazard of severe heat during summer for silkworm rearing.

## Skilled Workers

Unlike other crops sericulture needs special skill and

techniques. There is shortage of skilled labour. The requirement of skilled labour is essential to maintain timely feeding with required quantity and quality of leaves and also to safe, guard from pests. As sericulture is showing a progressive trend in the State, the provision for the availability of skilled workers must be promoted through imparting required skills periodically by the department of sericulture in the district.

## Cocoon Price Fluctuations

During the period of survey, it was found that the price of cocoons ranged between Rs. 60 and Rs. 80 per kilogramme of cocoons. The sericulturists are forced to sell the cocoons within ninth and tenth day for the price prevailing in the market undermining their income. In addition to this, the reelers also have the obligation to undertake reeling work immediately. To obviate these pressures, stifling units can be established by the government or private entrepreneurs. So that the cocoons may be stream stifled making the worm die in the cocoon. The cocoons can be preserved for a long time extending over months. This type of processing and preservations helps the sericulturists to realise better prices. The increase in the output of cocoons and raw silk should not be allowed to decrease the price of cocoons, through manipulation by the middle men. Fixation of cocoon and raw silk floor price is an essential ingredient of a package policy necessary to sustain the growth of sericulture in the State.

## Inadequate Market Facilities

Lack of proper marketing facilities constitute the main obstacle for the rapid development of sericulture in the district. Sericulturists have to send the cocoons to the Karnataka State every time for disposal. In the existing practice, in Karnataka regulated markets, cocoons are purchased by the dealers in an open auction system in a visual examination of the lots. Due regard is not paid to the quality of cocoons anywhere. The problems which sericulturists are facing in the Karnataka markets are mostly in the loss of sample cocoons supplied to the brokers, absence of proper weighing and unnecessary deduction of certain percentage on the plea that the produce is of inferior quantity. Moreover, the market costs vary from place to place depending on the distance and problems of transport.

At present there are five regulated markets in the district one each at Kadiri, Hindupur, Dharamvaram, Penukonda and Anantapur. Sericulturists from other mandals have to bring the cocoons to these markets facing difficulties of transportation, physical strain etc. Some of the rearers take the cocoons to Karnataka to get their prices, so efficient marketing organisation either through regulated markets or private dealers is an important necessity to be tackled on priority basis in building up an appropriate structure, creation of proper marketing facilities economise the cost of cocoon transportation and eradicate the incidental difficulties, sufficient number of markets may stimulate reeling activity and thereby promotes silk industry, in the region so as to generate more income and employment in the district.

## Extension Service

The sericulture department field officers are required to pay frequent visits to the sericulturists to guide them in their work, to check diseases as and whey they are detected and to direct them to cultivate better variety of mulberry with proper application of manure and fertilizer and watering and to make them adopt cross breed races of silkworms and better methods of rearing. Speedy growth of sericulture postulates intensive extension service to facilitate healthy innovation. The survey reveals that only 36.67 per cent of sericulturists could get access to the department extension service. Availability of adequate extension staff is one requirement and their dedicated service is most essential. In any case, speedy growth of sericulture involving innovations on the part of the farmers will not be feasible without the establishment of a competent extension service department which has to enlighten and advice the small farmers.

## Conclusion

As sericulture in the district is leading towards prosperity, the problems expressed by the farmers hinder the progress of sericulture. New farmers may hesitate to take up this activity, because of these problems involve. Hence, the department of sericulture should pay adequate attention to solve these problems. Otherwise, it will affect the development of sericulture in the district and those who have already engaged in sericulture activity may withdraw and switch over to the cultivation of other crops the yield of which may not be as increasing as that of the sericulture.

# 6

# Summary and Conclusion

Agriculture is the largest sector in Indian economy. It is providing not only food and raw materials but also employment to the vast population in India. Since agriculture reached a stage where it cannot absorb any increase of labour force because of large-scale unemployment and under-employment there is a need to develop agro-based industries to divert the surplus population from agriculture. Thus, sericulture is best suited to a country like India where there is surplus manpower and land resources besides its remunerative nature. By creating more employment opportunities to the rural population, sericulture prevents rural migration and also promotes handlooms sector.

The main objective of the study is to evaluate the growth and development of sericulture in Anantapur district and also to analyse the causative factors for the development of sericulture in the district.

Though India has attained the unique position of being the only country in the world which produces all the commercially known varieties of silk, over 90 per cent of silk produced in India is mulberry silk only. Further, mulberry silk production is better organised and is steadily increasing both in terms of acreage and also yields. With the liberal financial allocation in the Five Year Plans to promote this activity and the contribution of sericulture department through its research, sericulture, which was confined only to the States of Karnataka, West Bengal and Jammu and Kashmir, has spread to Andhra Pradesh and other States. Andhra Pradesh ranks second after Karnataka in production of mulberry raw silk in the country.

By the end of 1989 in Andhra Pradesh, 5,998 hectares of land was under mulberry cultivation and the production of reeling cocoons was of the order of 245.78 lakh kgs. There has been steep increase in the acreage and also production of raw silk in Rayalaseema region. But the cultivation of mulberry is mainly concentrated in Anantapur and Chittoor districts of Rayalaseema which together account for 64.39 per cent of the total area under mulberry cultivation in Andhra Pradesh.

Sericulture in Anantapur district has gained momentum in recent years. With the introduction and implementation of DPAP, IRDP and liberal financial support from the nationalised banks, Anantapur district has occupied unique place in the production of mulberry silk in the State. The district has advantage in terms of having favorable climatic conditions for the mulberry crop and rearing of silk worms.

Since the inception of DPAP, the area under mulberry cultivation has been increasing rapidly. The area which was 1,214 hectares under sericulture in 1975-76 has increased to 31,235 hectares by the end of March 1992. At present sericulture industry has been providing employment to 50,648 families in the district. Out of the total 50,648 families, the share of forward caste people is 54.54 per cent, while backward classes occupy second place with 35.22 per cent and the rest are Scheduled Caste and Scheduled Tribes.

Regarding employment opportunities in sericulture, it can be categorised under two heads. One is relating to the employment opportunities in the mulberry cutivation and silkworm rearing which are agriculture and are undertaken in rural areas and the other is silk reeling, twisting, weaving and marketing, which can be undertaken mostly in semi-urban and urban areas.

Analysis of comparative advantage of sericulture with other traditional crops in Anantapur district shows that employment opportunities and net returns from sericulture are higher return and employment throughout the year to the small and marginal farmers. It makes the ideal use of manpower, water and land resources as they are critical inputs in drought-prone regions.

The sericulture sector is beset with problems viz., availability of disease free layings in adequate quantity, occurrence of disease by pests, climatic hazards, paucity of funds and lack of skilled and trained workers and inadequate and insufficient marketing conditions for cocoons. It is heartening to note that sericulturists in the district could apply their minds and have achieved a significant progress in this direction..

Sericulture in the district is confronted with the problems of shortage of layings during summer season. There is an overall scarcity of seed during this season because the basic seed farms and seed areas and production of cocoons for eggs are inadequate. So even in summer, adequate quality of seed must be made available to relieve the farmers from the pain of going to the neighboring State.

Another important problem, which has been hindering the development of sericulture in the district, is the scarcity of labour. Because of inadequate training facilities, the supply of skilled labour is not sufficient to satisfy the demand for skilled labour. Hence, training facilities for sericulturists should be made available at all mandal headquarters.

Disease and pests and fluctuations in climate create a major problem and caused discontent among the sericulture farmers. Uzy fly, Grosserie, Flacherie and Pebron diseases, once affected, destroy the cocoon crop. Hence, sericulturists should be educated and provided with the necessary equipment to prevent the pests and diseases.

Another serious problem for the sericulture activity is the wide fluctuation in cocoon prices. This is because of the instability of cocoon crop and variations in the quality of cocoons. Inadequate marketing facilities are also a major reason for cocoon price fluctuations. The government should increase the number of regulated markets in the district. Due to inadequate market facilities, some sericulturists are marketing their cocoons in Bangalore. Unless steps are taken to have effective marketing organisation to prevent wide fluctuations in the price of cocoons, farmers will not have assured income.

Despite these problems there is a tremendous scope for the development of sericulture in Anantapur district both by way of expansion of sericulture in new areas and also modernising the activity which is already under operation in the district.

Further, a comprehensive programme has to be chalked out to provide training facilities to the sericulturists in the methods of silkworm rearing and maintaining equipment and also to educate the farmers about the necessity of maintaining suitable humidity and temperature and proper hygienic conditions. The training and extension centres have to be established at mandal level to conduct orientation programmes to the farmers. The programmes of this type are aimed to reduce the incidence of disease to silkworms and to get higher yields of cocoon crops.

Efforts have to be made to increase the production of seed cocoons, establishment of adequate number of grainages sufficient financial assistance to the farmers to increase the irrigation facilities, construction of rearing sheds etc. As a predominant agricultural activity to generate more employment in rural sector in Anantapur district, stability is the vital need of sericulture. Government have to take steps to streamline cocoon markets so as to regulate the prices of cocoons in such way as to enable the farmers to realise the fortunes of this labour-intensive activity in Anantapur district.

To conclude, sericulture development plays an important role in upgrading social and economic conditions of the farmers in general and the marginal and small farmers, who are drawn mostly from weaker sections of the society, in particular. Keeping this view, the author recommends appropriate incentives and subsidies to the sericulturists in the district. The just and efficient marketing condition go a long way in bettering the conditions of sericulturists in the district.

# Bibliography

## Books

Agarwal, S.K., and others : *Agricultural Economics and Co-operation*, S. Chand & Co. Ltd., 1970, New Delhi.

American Corporation : *Encyclopaedia Americana*, Vol. 24, International Head Quarters, 575, Lextington Avenue, New York.

Benjamin, R.E., and others : *Economics of Agriculture*, S. Chand & Co., Ltd., 1989, New Delhi.

Bansil, P.C. : *Agricultural Problems of India*, Third Edition, Vikas Publishing House Private Limited, 1977, New Delhi.

Choudary, M.R. : *Indian Industries Development and Location*, Fourth edition, Oxford & IBH Publishing Company, 1970, New Delhi.

Central Silk Board : *Souvenir*, International Congress on Tropical Sericulture Practices (18–23) February, 1988, Bangalore; *Silkman's Companion, 1989.*

Central Sericulture Research and Training Institute : *Achievements of CSRTI*, Mysore; *CSRTI & its organisational Set-up, 1981*, Mysore.

Central Silk Board : *Statistical Biennial, 1988*; *Statistical Biennial, 1992.*

Deshmukh, V.L. : *Can poverty be removed from our Country?* Bharateeya Vikas, Vol. I, No. 2, October–December, 1980.

F.A.O. : *Mannual of Sericulture–1, Mulberry Cultivation, Rome; Mannual on Sericulture–2, Silkworm Rearing, Rome; Mannual on Sericulture–3, Silk Reeling, Rome.*

Ghosh, Alok : *Indian Economy, 1988–89, Its nature and Problems*, The World Press Private Ltd., 1988, Calcutta.

Ghosh, C.C. : *Silk Production and Weaving in India*, CSIR, 1949, New Delhi.

Gopalachar, A.R.S. : *3 Decades of Sericulture Progress*, Central Silk Board, 1978, Bangalore.

Giri, V.V. : *Jobs for Millions*, 1970.

Gyan Chand : *Population in Perspective, 1972.*

Hanumappa, H.G. : *Sericulture for Rural Development*, Himalaya Publishing House, 1986, Bombay.

Harpal Singh, Y. : *Project for the Development of Sericulture*, National Institute of Bank Management, Bombay.

Jha, D.N. : *Planning and Agricultural Development*, Vikas Publications, 1974, New Delhi.

Jolly, M.S. : *Appropriate Sericulture Techniques*, Director, International Centre for Training and Research in Tropical Sericulture, Mysore.

Dr. Krishna Swamy, S. : *Mulberry Cultivation in South India*, CSB, 1986, Government of India, Ministry of Textiles, Bangalore; *New Technology of Silkworm Rearing*, CSB, 1986, Government of India, Ministry of Textiles, Bangalore; *Improved Method of Rearing Young Age (Chawkie) Silkworms*, CSB, 1986, Government of India, Ministry of Textiles, Bangalore.

Myrdal, Gunnar : *Asian Drama—An Enquiry into the Poverty of Nations*, The Twentieth Century Fund Inc., Vol. 11, 1968, London.

Mukerji, N.G. : *Handbook of Sericulture*, Bengal Secretariat Book Department, Calcutta, 1906.

Mysore Silk Association : *Silkwork Rearing and Diseases of Silkworm*, Bangalore, 1956.

Nanavathi, B. Manilal : *The Indian Rural Problems*, Seventh Edition, Indian Society of Agricultural Economics, Bombay.

Narayana, D.L. : *Economics of Sericulture in Rayalaseema*, Technical Cell, S.V. University, 1979, Tirupati.

Naryana, D.L. : *Employment and Economic Growth*, 1970, Madhurai Kamaraj University, Madhurai.

Ramana, D.V. : *Economics of Sericulture and Silk Industry in India*, Deep and Deep Publications, New Delhi, 1987.

Rowley, R.C. : *Economics of Silk Industry*, P.S. King and Sons Ltd., London, 1919.

Tanaka, Y. : *Sericology*, Translated from Japanese into English by C.S.B., 1969.

Tazima, Y. : *Sericulture Industry in India*, CSB, Bombay. 1976

Ullal, S.R. and Narasimhana, M.N. : *Handbook of Practical Sericulture*, CSB, 1978, Bombay.

## Reports

Central Silk Board : *Souvenir*, International Congress on Tropical Sericulture Practices (18–23), Bangalore, February, 1988; Silkman's Companion, 1982; Statistical Biennial, 1988; Statistical Biennial, 1992.

F.A.O. : *Mannual of Sericulture–1*, Silkwork Rearing–Rome; *Mannual of Sericulture–2*, Silkwork Rearing–Rome; *Mannual of Sericulture–3*, Silkwork Rearing–Rome.

C.S.R.T.I. : *Seridoc*, A quarterly document of Sericulture Research, Vol. 4, No. 2 & 3, April & July, 1988.

Government of Andhra Pradesh : *Anantapur District Gazetteer; Block Plans 1980–81, Anantapur District*, Intensive Development of Block under the IRDP.

Government of Andhra Pradesh : *Census of India, 1981, Series 1 and 2 District Census Hand Book*, Anantapur, parts XIII–A & B; *Credit Plan for Sericulture in Andhra Pradesh*, Department of Handlooms and Textiles, 1978; *Deputy Director, Department of Sericulture*, Anantapur; *Director, Department of Sericulture*, Hyderabad; *District Plans under Drought Prone Areas Programme, Integrated Rural Development Programme and District Rural Development Agency Programme*, Anantapur District; *District Statistical Abstract*, Anantapur, 1987–88; *Drought Prone Areas Programme*, Project Report; *Hand Book of Statistics*, Chief Planning Officer, 1985–86, Anantapur; *Planning and Development of Backward Regions—A Case Study in Rayalaseema*, Vol. 1.

Indian Institute of Economics : *Techno-Economic Survey of the Potentialities for the Development of Sericulture Industry in Andhra Pradesh*, (Unpublished), 1972.

National Commission on Agriculture : *Report of the National Commission on Agriculture*, (Part–III). Crop Production Sericulture and Agriculture, New Delhi, 1976.

National Institute of Rural Development : *Block Plan in the District Frame, A Development Plan for Madakasira Block in Anantapur District*, Andhra Pradesh, 1979.

Reserve Bank of India : *Report of Financing the Crash Programme for the Development of Sericulture in Karnataka, 1974*, Bombay.

The Hindu : *Survey on Indian Agriculture, Year Book*, 1989.

Government of India : *Report on the Continuance of Protection to the Sericulture Industry*, Bombay, 1974.

## Papers

Abdul Najid : Dramatic Development in Andhra Sericulture, *Kurukshetra*, Vol. XVII, No. 6, October, 1978.

Arun Chandra, Guha : 'The Urgency of Cottage Industries', *Khadi Gramodyog*, The Journal of Rural Economics, Vol. XXV, No. 2, November, 1978.

Ashal, M.M. : 'Package and Practices for Mulberry Cultivation under Temperate Conditions', *Indian Silk*, Vol. 29, No. 2, June, 1990.

Badar Alam Iqba :, 'Agro-Industries—Key to Economic Prosperity', *Khadi Gramodyog*, The Journal of Rural Economics, Vol. XXI, No. 10, July, 1975.

Balasubramanian, V. : 'Sericulture as a High Employment Oriented Industry', *Indian Silk*, Vol. XXV, No. 6, October, 1986.

Benchamin, K.V. et. al. : 'Employment and Income Generation in the Rural Areas through Sericulture', *Indian Silk*, Vol. XXVI, No. 2, June, 1987.

C.S.R.T.I. : 'Mulberry Cultivation under rainfed conditions, A Challenge that should be met', *Indian Silk*, Vol. XXVI, No. 8, December, 1987.

Dandin, S.D. : 'Mulberry Cultivation under rainfed conditions' A Challenge that should be met', *Indian Silk*, Vol. XXVI, No. 1, December, 1987.

Dastagir, S.R. : 'Sericulture', *Land Bank* Journal, Vol. XVIII, June, 1980 issue. iv.

Dalta, R.K. : 'Progress and Prospects of Sericulture in India under the Central Sector, *Indian Silk*, Vol. XXV, No. 9, January, 1987.

Deshmuk, V.L. : Can poverty be removed from our country? *Bharateeya Vikas*, Vol. I, No. 2, October–December, 1980.

Editor : 'District Plan with 56.79 Crores', *Eenadu*, February 9, 1989; 'Influence of Sericulture in a Drought Prone Area', *Eenadu*, February 26, 1988; 'Sericulture gets a boost in Rayalaseema', *Indian Express*, October 14, 1988.

Mathur, S.K. : 'Cocoon based Handicrafts—An additional source of income', *Indian Silk*, Vol. XXVI, No. 5, September, 1987.

Muneer Basha, Md. : 'Swiss aid to the Mulberry Sericulture Development Project in Andhra Pradesh and Tamil Nadu', *Indian Silk*, Vol. XXVII, No. 3, July, 1988.

Nair, M.N.V. : 'Sericulture—It's Place in National Economics', *Indian Silk*, Vol. XXVI, No. 10, February, 1988.

Narayana, D.L. : 'Employment Generation Through Sericulture' *Khadi Gramodyog*, Vol. XXV, No. 3, December, 1978.

Pahurkar, J.F. : 'Sericulture in Andhra Pradesh All Set for a Big Leap', *Indian Silk*, Vol. XXVIII. No. 5, September, 1989.

Rao, N.N. : 'Economics of Sericulture', *Khadi Gramodyog*, Vol. XXVIII, June, 1977.

Sekharappa, M. et. al. : 'Management of Silkworm Rearing Doing the Summer', *Indian Silk*, Vol. XXVII, No. 12, April, 1989.

Subbarayudu, B. et. al., 'The Economics of Sericulture in an adoptive New area of Andhra Pradesh', *Indian Silk*, Vol. XXVIII, No. 5, September, 1989.

Siva Prakash, G.S. : 'National Sericulture Project, *Indian Silk*, Vol. XXVII, No. 12, April, 1989.

Sampath, J. : 'Sericulture shows the way to success and prosperity', *Indian Silk*, Vol. XXVII, No. 4, August, 1988.

Sengupta, K. : 'Problems of Developing Sericulture in the New Areas and how to overcome them', *Indian Silk*, Vol. XXVII, No. 5, September, 1988.

Swaminathan, M.S. : 'The Future of our Sericulture Industries', *Indian Silk*, Vol. XXVI, No. 12, April, 1988.

Vijayalakshmi, G.S. : 'Sericulture, the Queen of Rural Industry,' *Yojana*, Vol. XXIII, No. 21, November, 1979.

# Index